Paul: Mystic and Missionary

Paul: Mystic and Missionary

BERNARD T. SMYTH

ORBIS BOOKS
Maryknoll, New York 10545

The Catholic Foreign Mission Society of America (Maryknoll) recruits and trains people for overseas missionary service. Through Orbis Books Maryknoll aims to foster the international dialogue that is essential to mission. The books published, however, reflect the opinions of their authors and are not meant to represent the official position of the society.

Published in Great Britain as *Paul: The Man and the Missionary* by Darton, Longman & Todd Ltd, 89 Lillie Road, London SW61UD, England

U.S. Edition published 1980 by Orbis Books, Maryknoll, NY 10545

Typeset in Great Britain; printed and bound in the United States of America

Library of Congress Cataloging in Publication Data

Smyth, Bernard T
  Paul, mystic and missionary.

  Includes index.
  1. Paul, Saint, apostle. 2. Bible. N.T.
Epistles of Paul—Theology. I. Title.
BS2506.S58   1980   225.9'24   80-14041
ISBN 0-88344-380-5 (pbk.)

It is in point to notice also the structure and style of Scripture, a structure so unsystematic and various, and a style so figurative and indirect, that no one would presume at first sight to say what is in it and what is not. It cannot, as it were, be mapped, or its contents catalogued; but after all our diligence, to the end of our lives and to the end of the Church, it must be an unexplored and unsubdued land, with heights and valleys, forests and streams, on the right and left of our path and close about us, full of concealed wonders and choice treasures.

(Cardinal Newman, *Development of Christian Doctrine*)

Certainly, we who have come from the gentiles into the Church are particularly pleased to call to mind that noble and heroic man who gloried in his infirmities, that teacher of the gentiles in faith and truth who 'laboured more' than any of the other Apostles and who, by means of many letters, instructed not only those of God's people who lived in his own time but even those who were to follow. Gladly and with the eyes of faith do all in the City of God look up to this great man, this athlete of Christ who was by Him instructed and anointed, and with Him 'nailed to the cross', and through Him made glorious, this man 'made a spectacle to the world, and to angels and to men', who lawfully carried on a great conflict in the theatre of this world and strained forward to the prize of his heavenly calling. They rejoice to behold him rejoicing with those who rejoice and weeping with those who weep having 'conflicts without and anxieties within', 'desiring to depart and to be with Christ', longing to see the Romans that he might produce some results among them, also, as well as among the rest of the gentiles, jealous concerning the Corinthians and fearing in that jealousy lest their souls be seduced and they forget their chaste betrothal to Christ, a man having 'great sadness and continuous sorrow' in his heart concerning the Israelites, who, 'ignorant of the justice of God and seeking to establish their own, have not submitted to the justice of God', and denouncing not only with sorrow but with anguish those who have 'sinned before and have not repented of their uncleanness and immorality'.

(St Augustine, *City of God*, Book 14)

Contents

Acknowledgements

Except where otherwise indicated, biblical quotations are taken from the Jerusalem Bible © 1966 Darton, Longman & Todd Ltd and Doubleday & Co. Inc.

Preface

Winston Churchill once said that everybody should always be writing a long book, since it is a sure way of never being bored. I have found this profoundly true over the past few years.

Still, writing a book also involves something of the loneliness of the long-distance runner. It would be ungracious of me not to say here a word of thanks to those who have eased the loneliness or notably helped along the way.

First, in order of time, my thanks go to Mrs Maura Maher and Mrs Lilian Murphy, both of them experts, no doubt often with the aid of a crystal ball, in translating my handwriting into English. They typed and retyped the material with the charity, joy, peace and patience—especially patience—that St Paul extols in Galatians.

Next come Father Richard Steinhilber, former Superior General of my own Society, and Father Christopher Mangan of Dun Laoghaire. In the early laps their encouragement was invaluable. If there are those whom this book infuriates, much of the initial anger should go in that direction.

I am grateful also to Dr Daniel Duffy and Father Thomas Ganly for theological assessment; and to Fathers Thomas O'Reilly and Maurice Hogan for scriptural help. Also to Sister Sheila Lucey for her efforts, gentle but firm, to nudge me towards civilised English. And I cannot easily say how much help, both theologically and otherwise, I have received from the Most Rev. John Howe, formerly Bishop of Myitkyina, Burma.

A warm word of thanks also to Professor A. T. Hanson of Hull University. To receive the competent and courteous guidance of so eminent a scholar was both a pleasure and a privilege. Professor

Hanson bears, of course, no responsibility for whatever transgressions of scholarship may yet remain.

Finally, I am uniquely grateful to Paul of Tarsus who has so enriched my own life and without whose Letters the writing of this book would have run into considerable difficulties.

Bernard T. Smyth
St Columban's, Navan

Approximate Chronology of Paul's Life

AD
10......Birth
36......Conversion
36–7....Arabia
37–40...Damascus
40......Jerusalem visit
40–4....Tarsus
44–6....Antioch
46–9....First missionary journey
49......Council of Jerusalem
        Antioch confrontation with Peter
49–52...Second missionary journey
52–4....Antioch
54–7....Third missionary journey
58......Return to Jerusalem
        Arrest
58–60...Prisoner in Caesarea
61–3....House arrest in Rome
63–7....Spain? Rome? Elsewhere?
67–8....Death in Rome, tradition says that of martyr

Introduction: Paul Revisited

These reflections on St Paul have a very modest purpose. It will emerge more clearly if I say how and why they came to be written.

I think Santiago de Chile has the loveliest setting of any city I know in the world. The Andes, usually with a mantilla of snow, tower up gigantically just behind the city and the giants peep out at you unexpectedly along the city streets whenever there is a gap in the buildings. Especially at evening, when the sun turns the rock mountain into a shimmer of golden brown, the beauty has to be seen to be almost disbelieved.

In the early summer of 1972 I visited our Columban missionaries in Santiago and was present at a Convention at which the missionaries reviewed their life and apostolate. Chile then was intellectually an exciting place. I have never been in a place where ideas jostled each other so incessantly in ordinary conversation. The magazine kiosks—and they were legion in Santiago—seemed to me a microcosm of Chileno society. They shouted at you in a babel of voices—Marxist, Socialist, Christian, post-Christian, pornographic, near-Fascist. Whatever else you might favour or fear in Allende's Chile, there was certainly freedom to express every shade of opinion. Intellectually it was a noisy and even strident world.

Inevitably a great deal of this rubbed off on the missionaries in Chile. Persistently they kept asking themselves at the Convention the question what did it mean to be a Christian and a missionary in Chile in 1972. It would be an exaggeration to say that there were as many answers as there were missionaries. It would not be very much of an exaggeration. One topic that came in for considerable discussion was the spiritual life of the missionary priest. There was unanimous agreement that much of the spiritual luggage picked up in the seminary travelled poorly and needed very badly to be replaced. But replaced with what?

I think it is fair to say that the Convention didn't even pretend to know the answer to that question. Some elements in a renewed missionary spirituality they were sure of—Scripture, Community, Eucharist. But mostly it was an uncertain groping with few enough direction posts clearly visible.

The question, of course, is not new and is not confined to Chile. But the Convention in Chile sharpened my personal perplexity about something which had been long and uneasily in and out of my mind. I think it was during one of these debates, probably when I was absently looking out of the window and marvelling at sunset over the Andes, that an idea, not a very original idea, came to me. Why not go back for guidance to St Paul, the first and greatest of missionaries? Perhaps he would have something timeless and true to say to the missionary of today.

Back in Ireland I remembered, and in spite of the world, the flesh and the TV, I began dipping into Paul at night. What commenced as a chore soon became an addiction. I am now, I think, incurable. At least I hope so. I did not, indeed, find in St Paul tidy answers to preconceived questions. In fact I found him refreshingly untidy in most respects. I doubt if there is a more untidy author in literature. That is part of the charm of this immense man, in his own way as gigantic and unexpected as the mountains behind Santiago.

It is chiefly the untidiness of St Paul that has encouraged me to write these pages. There is gold in all that he wrote but often it is scattered carelessly around, grains here, nuggets there. One of the features of Paul's writings is the way the sublime so often rubs shoulders with the trivial. A good example is Chapters 15 and 16 of I Corinthians. He has just been writing in Chapter 15 some of the most sublime things ever written about the Resurrection of Christ and our resurrection—Paul of course doesn't seriously distinguish between the two. And then, without pausing for breath, he goes on, 'Now about the collection.' That is Paul. To read him is to travel in the realms of gold. But the gold is found all over the place in huge clay-chunks of the prosaic.

As I explored the Pauline mine again and again, his thought patterns seemed to emerge more clearly. What he wrote in, for instance, I Thessalonians tied up with something in the Acts of the Apostles or found a climax in Ephesians. I came to see, or at least to imagine I could see, the general direction of some of the veins of gold. It was absorbing and rewarding. But it took time, more time than can readily be found by many a busy priest or apostolic Christian who, like myself, is far from being a Scripture scholar. It is for these only that I write, and even to them I merely point saying: 'Here, or so at least it seems to this prospector, one can hopefully dig for gold. Care to try?' For I am, as I have said, an addict. Any addict worth his salt, or his fix, will look around for new addicts who, in this context, might just take a hand in this digging for gold.

As I have just said, I am not a Pauline scholar, not even a Scripture scholar. This I regret, for, obviously, genuine scholarship would help enormously. But then on the other hand an accomplished Scripture scholar probably couldn't be bothered pointing out the simple obvious things about Paul which are the subject matter of these pages. His or her erudition might easily take for granted a great deal of what you and I need to be reminded of. It is a little bit like Shakespeare. One can revel in Shakespeare without being a Shakespearian scholar. It is similarly possible for us ordinary Christians to revel in Paul and drink in the great themes that dominated his mind while also accepting that we have much indeed to learn from those who have set themselves the hard professional task of opening to us the Scriptures as Christ himself did on the road to Emmaus.

All that I have sought to say in this rambling introduction could be summed up in a few lines from Kierkegaard,

My preaching is as though someone should say: what a wonderful sight the starry heavens are! And if those thousands of men were ready to listen to his words and say to him, 'What do you wish us to do, do you wish us to learn your discourse by heart?' must he not reply, 'No, no, no, but I want every single one of you to look up at the night starry heaven and each in his own way—and he can do it—be uplifted by the sight.'*

Throughout these pages, Paul is the starry heaven and the sight.

Even in a book like this, reflective rather than scholarly, it is right to say what Pauline Letters are treated as authentic. Following a wide stream of reliable scholarship, I treat as authentic the Letters to Thessalonika and Corinth; Philippians, Galatians, Romans, Philemon, Colossians—and probably Ephesians. Scholarship is more divided over the Pastoral Letters, I and II Timothy and Titus, and the arguments against authenticity are important. It seems better not to assume their authenticity here but to use them, with caution, for the valuable insights they often give into Paul's thought, work and life.

---

*Søren Kierkegaard, *The Last Years: Journals 1853–5*, ed. and tr. by R. Gregor Smith (Collins Fontana 1965).

PART ONE

Paul and Turmoil

Chapter I

TRAVEL AND TUMULT

In retrospect, as in his life, it is hard to pin Paul down; and it is impossible to place him in a single category. He was a passionate Jew and yet a cosmopolitan citizen of the wider world of Greece and Rome. He was a formidable opponent and controversialist; but he was gently persuasive and diplomatic when pleading for a runaway slave. He could be a trenchant and blunt critic when the opposition of Jews or the shortcomings of Christians demanded it. Yet of his Jewish brethren he could write, 'I would willingly be condemned and cut off from Christ if it could help my brothers of Israel, my own flesh and blood' (Romans 9:3). And, no matter how backsliding or infuriating his Christians might be, no matter how angry and almost savage Paul might be in reprimanding them, in the end his attitude to them was that of his Letter to the Philippians, 'You have a permanent place in my heart; and God knows how much I miss you all, loving you as Christ Jesus loves you' (Philippians 1:7–8). He was a daring innovator and yet, as in Galatians, angrily conservative when it came to what today we should call questions of orthodoxy, 'if anyone preaches a version of the Good News, different from the one you have already heard, he is to be condemned' (Galatians 1:9). He was man of action and travel by nature, writer and near-poet by necessity and almost by accident. By teaching, as he constantly did, that all human beings, slaves or free, Jews or Greeks, men or women were equal before God, he probably did more, in the long term, for the elevation of womanhood than any other human being with the exception of the Mother of God. And yet he has infuriated the women of many generations, notably our own, by his irritable outbursts here and there in his

3

Letters, outbursts clearly keeping women in what he saw as their place. He was Apostle, as was Xavier; theologian in the category of Aquinas, even though he was an embryonic and untidy theologian; mystic as was John of the Cross. A phrase of his own sums him up better than perhaps he guessed when he wrote it, 'I made myself all things to all men, in order to save some at any cost; and I still do this, for the sake of the gospel, to have a share in its blessings' (I Corinthians 9:22–3).

In respect of a man so various, one must start somewhere. As good a starting-point as any other is the turmoil of his life.

*

Paul was a man who had to go where it was happening. Nearly always we find him in the crowd scenes, usually at the centre of them, often the cause of the tumult and the riot. There were no sociologists on the scene in those days earnestly filing away human behaviour. But if there had been a sociologist around then, particularly one specialising in riots, I imagine that Paul's monthly output in riots would compare favourably with any competitor of his generation.

Take Chapter 9 of the Acts of the Apostles. If you read verses 30–1 you are forced to the conclusion that the author, probably Luke, either had a tremendous deadpan sense of humour or no sense of humour at all. Paul was in Jerusalem and typically couldn't be stopped from broadcasting his new beliefs. In no time at all he had become too hot to handle; there was even a plot by the Hellenists against his life. Luke goes on, 'When the brothers knew, they took him to Caesarea and sent him off to Tarsus. The churches throughout Judea, Galilee and Samaria were now left in peace.'

Apparently, you could have Paul or you could have peace. You couldn't easily have both.

Originally, I thought of calling this book *The Mystic of Tumult*—the title sums up for me much of Paul's life. The mystic—hardly any Christian will claim a deeper insight than he into 'the mystery of Christ'. But if he were merely a mystic he would be a very inadequate model for the missionary. Especially for the missionary of today who also has to be where the action is, action sometimes

4

ambiguous, disorderly, unpredictable, even violent. It can seem an impossible background for a sustained life of prayer and faith. But it is just out of that tumult that we hear the voice of Paul telling us, 'to me to live is Christ'. Because the voice comes from the tumult, not from a monastery, we can listen and find new heart. That is why I have thought it right to look in these initial chapters at the Storm of Event—the phrase, of course, is Dag Hammarskjöld's in *Markings*—which was the God-appointed setting of Paul's burning inner life.

There is no record that Paul ever went up to a mountain to pray. For that matter there is no record that he ever went up a mountain at all. Indeed one gets the impression that for him the countryside was a necessary evil between towns and cities. He was a people's priest, and the people, apparently, were mostly in the cities. His prayer grew not in the quiet of the monastery but amid the clamour of the mob. I think he would have felt very much at home in the urbanised society of our day.

It is entirely right that we first meet him (Acts 7:58) in a furious crowd scene; the crowd was stoning Stephen to death. That he had a leading part in it is quite clear. It was a memory not to fade. Some thirty years later he has just been arrested after a riot in the same city of Jerusalem which stoned Stephen to death and which now rings with the same cry about Paul, 'Kill him, kill him.' He gets leave to speak to the people, 'when the blood of your witness Stephen was being shed I was standing by in full agreement with his murderers and minding their clothes' (Acts 22:20). He couldn't forget. I expect it is not easy to forget an innocent man you have helped to murder, not even after half a lifetime.

Stephen was not the only Christian in whose death Paul had a share. How many others there may have been we don't know. But there were others: 'I myself threw many of the saints into prison . . . and when they were sentenced to death I cast my vote against them. . . . My fury against them was so extreme that I even pursued them into foreign cities' (Acts 26:10–11).

His reference to 'foreign cities' is intriguing. Foreign cities would mostly be the context of Paul's life. Even as a persecutor he was impatient of limits, one eye always beyond the immediate horizon. Until the end of his life he would remain one for the road.

5

It was of course on the road that Christ chose to meet and capture Paul. Paul wasn't on his own. He practically never was. How big was his retinue we don't know. But if your immediate objective is 'to arrest and take to Jerusalem any followers of the Way, men and women', that you can find, you would need help. So it is probably right to think of Paul at the head of a little army, as he approached Damascus and his destiny. And then it happened. The story is too well known to repeat it. The men travelling with him, we are told, stood speechless. It was a chaotic situation. So Paul's first effect as a Christian was to create chaos around about him. The habit would stick. Indeed a few paragraphs after Paul's conversion, Luke says, 'Saul's power increased steadily and he was able to throw the whole Jewish colony at Damascus into complete confusion' (Acts 9:22). Paul was good at that. And, arising from the confusion, the tumult and the chaos we find the worldwide Pauline journeys beginning rather humiliatingly by his being let down over a wall in a basket. God had put a lot of his eggs in one basket.

*

New Year's Day 1974 found me doing a six-hours' bus journey from Seoul, capital of South Korea, to visit my *confrères*, missionaries in and around Kwangju, a city far to the south. It was the first time I ever saw the great highways which now ribbon their way across South Korea and which make you almost think that you are in Germany or the USA. A radio at the back kept us entertained, if that is the right word, but as all of it was in Korean, it was lost on me. At one point, however, my travelling companion, a veteran of many years in Korea, pricked up his ears and some five minutes later, told me that the radio had just given an admirable summary of the Holy Father's New Year's message on peace. And the young conductress on the bus, whom I had admired earlier for keeping her temper with one or two difficult passengers, approached us shyly during the journey and asked my companion if he was a Catholic priest. When he said, 'Yes,' she smiled and said she was a Catholic too. Immediately there was a new intimacy. Being Korean or Irish was irrelevant in comparison with all that we shared. Paul must have felt much the same during his 'journeyings

6

often' when some deckhand or slave girl told him in a whisper that he or she, too, was a follower of the Way.

The bus was very full indeed, full of passengers and crammed down towards the back with luggage. For the New Year in Korea is *the* time for going home, and half Korea was on the move these days. A few of the Koreans had Western-style suitcases but they were very much the minority. The rest had packed all they needed—clothes, presents, cookery utensils, probably food—into a huge shapeless bag-like cloth, had rolled the cloth up into a shape rather like an untidy tar barrel and then had somehow squeezed it on board the bus. That was where the Christian conductress came in, trying to point out the physical limitations of the bus. But the Koreans didn't take much notice either of her or the limitations. Somehow they found or made space, smiled at a conductress admitting defeat and then, for the most part, happily settled down and went to sleep in spite of the radio.

This Korean memory has left me with a picture, accurate or inaccurate, of Paul on his journeyings. I imagine him with a great roll-up container like those I saw in Korea. In it would be his clothes, no doubt including the cloak he left with Carpus in Troas; scrolls, parchment and writing materials; maybe the tools, whatever they were, needed in his trade of tent making. After all, every tradesman likes his own tools. I should hate to be a conductress on a bus or a boat trying to explain to Paul that there really wasn't room for so huge a bundle. I don't think Paul would listen very patiently. I doubt if in any circumstances he was a good listener. If he was, the evidence hasn't survived.

But whether or not the mental picture is accurate, there is no doubt about the journeyings. 'From Jerusalem to Illyricum'—that is how he describes them with an endearing touch of vanity towards the end of his Letter to the Romans written perhaps in AD 58. (Is he thinking a little impishly of stay-at-home Apostles in Jerusalem?) That same Chapter 15 of Romans, as it tells of Paul's travel plans, reads like an hour in an airline office. 'Yes,' it says, 'I'm here in Corinth and I have in mind a trip to Spain. But in the meantime I have some financial business in Jerusalem to attend to. After that I hope to make a stopover in Rome on the way to Spain. See you then.' That was Paul's life once he started on the missionary trail.

7

The great missionary command begins, 'Go teach.' Paul certainly went. There were interludes—one in Ephesus for two or three years, a shorter one in Corinth. But Paul was normally on the road. He was rather like a Jumbo Jet. He would touch down now and again but by nature, vocation and grace he was made to travel.

Paul's life was always crowded, frequently exciting, occasionally hectic, now and then frantic. In short, a life of tumult. And a life of controversy. The controversy was sometimes with those inside the Church, sometimes with those outside it. Paul, the preacher of Christ's peace, is normally found in the middle of a heated argument, sometimes just short of boiling point. Often enough the argument developed into a riot. I have a general impression that in any given city after Paul's arrival, the gestation period from argument to riot was about three weeks.

Was Paul then almost a professional agitator, constantly in search of conflict and confrontation? Paul is indeed sometimes so portrayed, particularly by those who naively see Christianity chiefly as a tearing down of structures, a non-stop rebellion against the *status quo*. Any such picture of Paul cannot survive a serious look at the evidence. He was, it is true, very often in conflict and confrontation. But this was unsought. We can authentically place on his lips the clear simple statement by the other Apostles, 'We must obey God rather than man.' If this meant trouble, then, but regretfully, let trouble be.

The evidence for this is, I think, overwhelming. One can offer only a few illustrations. When he writes to Rome we find, 'You must obey all the governing authorities . . . all government comes from God, the civil authorities were appointed by God' (Romans 13:1). In Ephesians and Colossians he tells slaves quite bluntly that they are to obey their masters. In his First Letter to the Thessalonians, probably the earliest of his extant Letters, he spells out the Christian attitude to those rightfully exercising Christian leadership, 'be considerate to those who are working amongst you and are above you in the Lord as your teachers. Have the greatest respect and affection for them because of their work' (I Thessalonians 5:12–13). And the record clearly shows that Paul, wherever he went, courteously sought out and tried to win over the Jews to Christ. If their opposition ultimately became a riot, at least Paul had tried.

Paul, the incurable and incorrigible rebel against authority may be attractive to certain temperaments. It is not Paul of Tarsus: Paul's radicalism was far deeper than mere rebelliousness. It went to the roots of God's relationship with man.

*

For about ten years or more after the Damascus conversion we have only limited information on Paul's life. He pops up in Damascus, Arabia, Syria, Cicilia and briefly in Jerusalem. Whatever the details of facts, dates and places, one thing emerges clearly. As far as the leadership of the Christian Church was concerned, Paul was left out in the cold. The Apostles had chosen Matthias to replace Judas. They probably didn't quite know what to make of Paul or what to do with him. It must have been some relief to them that he was carrying on his freelance apostolate in Cicilia and Arabia, comfortably far away from Jerusalem. When Paul tells us in the Letter to the Galatians that on his visit to Jerusalem he stayed only fifteen days, it is easy to surmise that Peter didn't insist too much on a longer stay. It was Peter's experience, no doubt, that wherever you had Paul you had trouble. And Peter had enough trouble on his hands without Paul around, insisting rather too loudly that there was no longer Jew or gentile but that all were one in Christ Jesus. Anyhow for Paul it was a decade under a cloud because he was theologically ahead of his time.

Quite suddenly the cloud lifted and in a very human sort of way. During Paul's visit to Jerusalem around AD 40, Barnabas had acted as Paul's patron and introduced him to the Apostles in spite of the widespread suspicion that Paul was a spy infiltrating the Christian community. Five years later the Apostles sent Barnabas up to Antioch (not all that far from Tarsus, perhaps 150 miles) to look into a disturbing rumour that the Christian Gospel was being freely preached, and quite successfully at that, not only to Jews but to pagans as well. Barnabas found the rumour to be accurate. But far from disapproving, he was most impressed by the evidence of God's grace poured out just as richly on pagan people. It is interesting to speculate whether his association with Paul in Jerusalem had helped to prepare his mind for just this explosive possibility. Anyhow, he now thought of Paul. It is even conceivable that Barnabas wanted somebody like Paul as an ally in the argument with people back in Jerusalem. So off he went in search of him. Last heard of in Tarsus; could be anywhere. Somewhere, quite possibly in Tarsus itself, Barnabas found Paul and brought him back as a helper to Antioch. Paul had come out of the cloud and his real life's work was about to begin.

Chapter II

'MY CHOSEN INSTRUMENT'
(Acts 9:15)

Paul had many roles. He had only one vocation. He was traveller, writer, exegete, theologian, mystic, missiologist, preacher, organiser, critic, lover. But these were only aspects of his one and only vocation: to be an Apostle to the gentiles.

In Paul's mind there was no iota of doubt about his special vocation to the gentiles. How could there be? In very large measure Paul himself must have been the source of the traditions that we find gathered up concerning him by the author of Acts. In Acts we find that Paul's conversion to Christianity and his call to apostolate are hardly distinguishable. In the first account of the conversion, the Lord says to Ananias, 'this man is my chosen instrument to bring my name before pagans and pagan kings and before the people of Israel' (Acts 9:15).

In the second account, God tells Paul, through Ananias, that he has chosen him 'to be his witness before all mankind, testifying to what you have seen and heard' (Acts 22:15). A few verses later Christ himself speaks to Paul in a vision, 'Go, I am sending you to the pagans far away' (Acts 22:21). In the third account of the conversion Paul's vocation to apostolate among the gentiles is clearer then ever, 'I have appeared to you for this reason: to appoint you as my servant and as witness of this vision in which you have seen me and of others in which I shall appear to you. I shall deliver you from the people and from the pagans to whom I am sending you' (Acts 26:16–17). If the Paul of Acts is the Paul of history, there is no doubt what his automatic self-image was: Apostle to the gentiles.

11

But if this was axiomatic for Paul it was less obvious to others. Even the other Apostles, Peter among them, had their reservations. It is not too clear if the reservations ever fully disappeared. Paul had plenty of other critics to cast doubt upon his claim to be an Apostle, on a par with the other Apostles; and, even more, to have received from the Lord a special commission given to none of them—to be the Apostle to the gentiles. The critics had an impressive case. Christ had chosen twelve Apostles to be uniquely heralds of the Good News and witnesses of the Resurrection, and Matthias had replaced Judas. Christ had never given any hint of another. And this Paul? A rather odd candidate, to begin with; and, apart from his uncorroborated and rather improbable story, what evidence was there that he had ever seen the Lord? On the whole then—so the argument seems to have run among Paul's critics—isn't it a reasonable assumption that these pretensions of Paul to be an Apostle are due to a touch of megalomania?

These doubts were widespread and persistent. They are the background to Paul's strident claim throughout his writings that he is in all truth an Apostle, on a par with the others, and in some ways above par. There are only four of his Letters which do not begin with a loud assertion of this claim—the two Letters to Thessalonika, that to Philippi, and the personal Letter to Philemon. In the Letters to Thessalonika, Paul is quite content to put himself on a level with non-apostles: 'From Paul, Silvanus and Timothy to the Church in Thessalonika' (I Thessalonians 1:1 and II Thessalonians 1:1). This is understandable. It is early in Paul's apostolate. The problem of the authenticity of his apostleship has not yet widely arisen. Philippians belongs to a later period, when the question certainly loomed large, but this is essentially a farewell letter (even if the farewell was tentative) to loyal friends entertaining no doubt about Paul's claim to apostolate. So there was no particular need to reaffirm it. But in all the other Letters, Paul begins by trumpeting his claim to be 'a servant of Christ Jesus who has been called to be an apostle and specially chosen to preach the Good News that God promised long ago through his prophets in the scriptures' (Romans 1:1–2).

Nowhere does he trumpet it quite so angrily as in Galatians. 'The troublemakers among you who want to change the Good News of Christ' had challenged his claim to be an Apostle and Paul replies with no small voice. Even though he seems to be a late arrival, 'Then God, who had specially chosen me while I was still in my mother's womb, called me through his grace ... so that I might preach the Good News about him to the pagans' (Galatians 1:15–16).

With this choice and call clear from Damascus, Paul, sure of his unique vocation, experienced no need for human intermediaries, 'I did not stop to discuss this with any human being, nor did I go up to Jerusalem to see those who were already apostles before me, but I went off to Arabia at once and later went straight back from there to Damascus' (Galatians 1:16–17). Apostles before me! Not Apostles who might, as in the case of Matthias, co-opt Paul. Rather Apostles who, like it or not, must consider Paul as an Apostle on a footing of equality with themselves. As he would put it later in writing to Corinth, 'Am I not an apostle? Have I not seen Jesus Our Lord?' Paul is in emphatic agreement with Peter about one indispensable prerequisite for authentic apostolate, 'he can act with us as a witness to the resurrection' (Acts 1:22). Paul claimed to have met and spoken to the risen Lord; to have been sent by him. No doubt he asked whether anybody could claim more. If he were genuinely Apostle neither could he claim less. He simply had to be witness of the Resurrection.

A genuine Apostle, even though independent of the other Apostles, could *consult* with them. In Galatians Paul tells us that he did just that. Even so slight a step, however, he was reluctant to take. When he went up to Jerusalem taking Barnabas and Titus with him he 'went there as a result of a revelation' (Galatians 2:2). He was as reluctant as that. Still go he did and 'laid before the leading men the Good News as I proclaim it among the pagans' (Galatians 2:2). The leaders in Jerusalem 'had nothing to add to the Good News as I preach it' (Galatians 2:6). There was agreement, apparently, that just as Peter had been appointed by Christ as chief Apostle to the Jews, so Paul had been appointed by the same Christ as chief Apostle to the gentiles. So at least Paul understood it; but there is a remarkable lack of corroboration in the New Testament. So James, Cephas and John shook hands with Barnabas and Paul, wishing them God speed on their journeys to the gentiles. It has Old Testament echoes of Abraham and Lot, one choosing

13

the right and other the left. From Peter's point of view it must have been, to put it as its lowest level, an acceptable working arrangement likely to keep the choleric Paul comfortably far away from Jerusalem. But at a deeper level Peter was probably glad to hand over the gentile apostolate to Paul who knew his way so well around the cosmopolitan Graeco-Roman world. There is no evidence that Peter, up to this point, had ever been outside Palestine. Paul had been far and wide. He was probably the only one of the Apostles who could have read Pilate's inscription on the Cross in Hebrew, Greek and Latin; and from a human point of view was better equipped to carry the Good News along the Roman roads.

But there was another and perhaps more important reason why Paul should keep returning to Christ's choice of him as Apostle of the gentiles. When burdens became unbearable or opposition became intolerable—and that was a lot of the time—it was an immensely comforting thought to go back to: that he had not chosen this work but God had chosen him for it. He returns to this thought so constantly as to make it clear that this was one of the great sources of his strength. 'I became the servant of the Church when God made me responsible for delivering God's message to you' (Colossians 1:25). The thought comes automatically in even when Paul is talking about something entirely different, e.g. money, 'If I had chosen this work myself, I might have been paid for it but as I have not, it is a responsibility which has been put into my hands' (I Corinthians 9:17). The author of I Timothy surely tells us something true and intimate about Paul in the cry of gratitude he puts on Paul's lips near the end. 'How I thank our Lord Jesus Christ, the source of all my strength, for showing confidence in me by appointing me his minister' (I Timothy 1:12. Knox). *The source of all my strength!*' God's clear call and commission were things to go back to when skies were dark.

*

Paul then sees himself as authentic messenger from God. What were the human qualities and the providential background of this messenger?

First the providential background. The most obvious point about it was that Paul, having grown up at Tarsus, in the Graeco-Roman world, was a citizen of that world, speaking its languages, understanding its outlook and customs, therefore feeling at home in that world and able to speak to it in a way that might be understood. But, since Paul's mission was to be a *religious* mission, it is right to see Paul's most important preparation taking place, not so much in areas of language and culture, however important these might be, but rather somewhere in the area of religion. Paul was a Jew just as much (to take a few quick examples) as were Zachary, Simeon or Anna in the Temple. In fact he was a particularly strict sort of Jew, 'a Hebrew born of Hebrew parents, and I was circumcised when I was eight days old. As for the Law, I was a Pharisee' (Philippians 3:5–6). And yet he was a Jew in so different a context that, inevitably, this context made him a Jew very different in outlook from Zachary, Simeon or Anna. These lived in or near Jerusalem where everybody, more or less, was a Jew; where Judaism was the air you breathed. There were gentiles around, of course, but they were the exception. In Tarsus it was just the opposite. The Jewish community there was a ghetto clinging to its own view of life in the face of gentile presuppositions and ways. Paul, growing up in this gentile milieu where Jewish assumptions were constantly challenged, must have been very conscious of other views of life, views irreconcilable with his Jewish faith. The result was, apparently, to turn Paul into a Jew still more convinced, even bigoted, 'you must have heard of my career as a practising Jew, how I stood out among other Jews of my generation, and how enthusiastic I was for the traditions of my ancestors' (Galatians 1:13–14). Enthusiastic, yes. But it was an enthusiasm aware of, forged in and tempered by the great surrounding, uncaring and slightly contemptuous gentile consensus illustrated unconsciously by Gallio, pro-consul in Achaia,

Listen you Jews. If this were a misdemeanour or a crime, I would not hesitate to attend to you; but if it is only quibbles about words or names, and about your own Law, then you must deal with it yourselves—I have no intention of making legal decisions about things like that (Acts 18:14–15).

15

In this world of contemptuous dismissal Paul grew up. He remained faithful to the traditions of his ancestors in spite of that world. But he must have been very much aware of, probably at times attracted by, views irreconcilable with Judaism; a Judaism which, indeed, probably sometimes seemed narrow and constricting to an intelligent young Jew, beginning to reflect on his world. Life flung at him disturbing questions that never, one imagines, had troubled the serenity of Zachary, Simeon, or Anna. Paul, destined to fashion new answers for Jew and gentile, almost had to grow up bothered by the questions. Tarsus took care of that.

To judge by the evidence, slender but significant, of Paul's Letters his reservations about Judaism had run deep. Romans, mainly theology, is also part autobiography. 'Failing to recognise the righteousness that comes from God, they try to promote their own idea of it, instead of submitting to the righteousness of God' (Romans 10:3). It had been Paul's mistake too. His vision, getting lots of the details quite right, had got the whole picture all wrong. The emphasis was far too much on rules to be observed, far too little on love and mercy to be accepted as pure gift. This mistaken emphasis had led to frustration, turmoil and near desperation, 'What a wretched man I am! Who will rescue me from this body doomed to death?' (Romans 7:24.) Already as a young Jew, Paul, it is fairly obvious, felt at least dimly that even though Judaism had many answers it did not have the final answer. It was splendid but incomplete. Whether or not he realised it at the time, the scepticism of the world about him in Tarsus and his own inner experience had combined to open Paul's mind and heart to possibilities even richer than the Judaism he treasured so fiercely.

For he did treasure it fiercely and served it loyally. Whatever the misgivings thrust upon him by a hostile environment or born in him from experience of the human struggle, it was the highest ideal he knew and he was untiring and even cruel in its service; uncompromising in opposition to whatever seemed to threaten the foundations of Judaism. He was clear sighted enough to see that this Jesus from Galilee, and especially those spreading the absurd story of his Resurrection, did pose a serious threat.

. . . I once thought it was my duty . . . to oppose the name of Jesus, the

16

Nazarene. This I did in Jerusalem. I myself threw many of the saints into prison, acting on authority for the chief priests, and when they were sentenced to death I cast my vote against them . . . my fury against them was so extreme that I even pursued them into foreign cities. On one such expedition I was going as far as Damascus . . . (Acts 26:9–12).

What were some of the human qualities God gave to Paul to prepare him for apostolate? The first overall impression is of a man of great conviction and dedication, with an immense need of an ideal to serve. Paul could never be happy, indeed could not be Paul, and settle for a comfortable, undemanding life. A need for an ideal: and something inside him drove him to total self-giving in the service of that ideal. This was true of his Jewish days, 'how I stood out among all other Jews of my generation, and how enthusiastic I was for the traditions of my ancestors' (Galatians 1:14). We recognise the same Paul in I Corinthians, 'So though I am not the slave of any man, I have made myself the slave of everyone to win as many as I could. I made myself . . . all things to all men in order to save some at any cost' (I Corinthians 9:19,22). He was the most reluctant convert in history and the most committed.

Secondly, he belonged to people. Paul, while he cared very much for ideas and loved to express them, could never be happy with ideas alone. He could not stand on the edge of the crowd and observe. He had to jump in and be part of it, preferably in the thick of it. This trait shows up both in the Jew and the Christian. As a young Jew, trained by Gamaliel and disturbed by the radical and dangerous teachings of the new sect springing up around Jesus from Galilee, he might have just argued against it. But that wasn't Paul. '. . . when the blood of your witness Stephen was being shed I was standing by in full agreement with his murderers, and minding their clothes' (Acts 22:20). It is just the same Paul, the Paul who must be up and at it, that we meet towards the end of Romans. By then his apostolic mileage must have been greater than that of all the other Apostles together and he recalls with pride his journeyings often, all the way from Jerusalem to Illyricum. But, not one to rest on his laurels or his mileage, in the next breath he is planning journeys to Macedonia, Achaia, Rome and eventually Spain. The first word in Christ's great missionary mandate is 'Go'. Paul cer-

17

tainly went. Not really, however, to places but to people. There is no evidence that Paul was greatly interested in Corinth, Ephesus, Rome or Galatia. He was intensely interested in Corinthians, Ephesians, Romans and Galatians.

But Paul, man of action, was not just activist. His restless activity was not divorced from and certainly not opposed to ideas. Indeed he was interested in action or travel only in so far as these served ideas and ideas served people. Romans is a good example. Both at the beginning of the Letter and towards its end travel is very much on Paul's mind. He tells the Romans, perhaps one should say warns them, that he will be along presently; and almost seems to reassure them that he won't stay too long before heading for Spain. In between we have fourteen chapters containing some of the most profound reflection there is on the ways of God with man. This make-up of Romans is a good enough image of Paul's life. If he were merely or mainly Paul of the mileage, what a pitifully poor Paul he would be!

Man of dedication, man of action, man of travel, man of ideas. But not superhuman. The Paul of the New Testament is very much a human being, quirky, mostly lovable, sometimes maddening, with limitations, obstinacies and oddities peculiarly his own. Rather quarrelsome by nature: violent rows with, among others, John Mark, Barnabas, Peter, Hymenaeus and Philetus, not to mention Alexander the coppersmith. Independent to the point of prickliness. Independent of the other Apostles. Rather quick to see what many might regard as a mote in Peter's eye; less conscious of what some might see as a beam or two in his own. Independent—or at least claiming to be—of the reaction of his converts to his teaching. Like it or leave it, he would keep telling them the truth about Christ, the whole truth and nothing but the truth, 'We do not, like so many others, adulterate the word of God, we preach it in all purity as God gave it to us standing before God's presence in Christ' (II Corinthians 2:17. Knox). Sensitive, almost jealous, about his own special relationship to those to whom he was the first to preach the Gospel, 'Yes, you may have ten thousand schoolmasters in Christ but only one father' (I Corinthians 4:15. Knox). Man of courage to whom difficulty and danger meant little or nothing, 'life to me is not a matter to waste words on' (Acts 20:24). The Second Letter to

Timothy gives us a picture, probably authentic, of Paul near the end, 'As for me, my life is already being poured away as a libation and the time has come for me to be gone' (II Timothy 4:6). The words attributed to Paul breathe an enviable serenity in the face of death; it may well be a picture from memory. Independent to the point of militancy–and yet a man desperately needing friendship and depending very much, perhaps more than he realised, on the affection of his friends. It emerges in a dozen places, nowhere more poignantly than in his Second Letter to Corinth:

> I may have hurt you, but if so I have hurt the only people who could give me any pleasure. I wrote as I did to make sure that, when I came, I should not be distressed by the very people who should have made me happy. I am sure you all know that I could never be happy unless you were (II Corinthians 2:2–3).

A man of changing moods, whose Second Letter to the Corinthians might have been written to illustrate how quickly Paul could change from acute depression to exhilaration. This is one of the reasons why some scholars suggest that II Corinthians is a compilation of several Letters, not a single one. One respects their scholarship and they may well be right. But one can also wonder if, at this particular level, it is right to attach great importance to consistency. The mercurial Paul of II Corinthians is far richer, in human terms, than (say) the careful author of Hebrews. I at any rate like to cling to a Paul who could be both so mad and so glad inside a single Letter, perhaps written over a couple of weeks, to a group of his special friends. And he regularly pays his friends the compliment of expecting a lot from them. Unceremoniously, and with no apology, he repeatedly tells them that he will be along soon and will expect accommodation. The best example of this trait is, of course, the tiny little Letter to Philemon. He does not ask, he practically demands that Philemon receive back as a brother the runaway slave Onesimus. In his attitude towards women there is a curious contradiction. Repeatedly he is acidic about women and critical of their behaviour. And yet when he sends special greetings, women figure prominently in the list. Perhaps, even then, women were more easily attracted to Christianity than men, and Paul, like

19

many after him, may have been wary of a female-dominated Church. There is no hint that he indulged in any recreation apart from the company of his friends,'reading to the people, preaching and teaching' (I Timothy 4:13). If this blueprint of the ideal missionary reflects Paul's mind, he didn't visualise much spare time in the lives of his helpers. But the same Letter, more humanly, encourages Timothy to take a little wine for his stomach's sake. Tireless worker himself, he hated idleness in others. As early as in II Thessalonians he rebukes 'some of you who are living in idleness, doing no work themselves but interfering with everyone else's' (II Thessalonians 3:11). Sensitive about criticism, especially the suggestion that he was making a good thing out of the Gospel; it is an important point to Paul and one to which I hope to return. He had some odd ideas, odd at least to us, about the implications of his special vocation to the gentiles.

There is the principle, alluded to in various places but unmistakably enunciated in Romans, 'I have always made it an unbroken rule never to preach where Christ's name has already been heard' (Romans 15:20). Perhaps this curious principle had something to do with Paul's concept of himself as a messenger who arrives, delivers the message and then hurries on to deliver it elsewhere. In spite of Christ's command to go and teach all nations, baptising them in the name of the Father and of the Son and of the Holy Spirit, Paul, as a general rule, did not, it would appear, himself baptise his converts. 'I never baptised any of you after Crispus and Gaius, so none of you can say he was baptised in my name. Then there was the family of Stephanus, of course, that I baptised too, but no one else as far as I can remember' (I Corinthians 1:14). Clearly he saw himself as Apostle essentially in the area of Word and only incidentally in the area of Sacrament. And minister of the Word Paul certainly was. About the only time we meet a muted Paul is at the stoning of Stephen when 'The witnesses put down their clothes at the feet of a young man called Saul' (Acts 7:59). After that it is normally Paul in full flow; if you like, Paul in eruption. When we next meet him he is 'still breathing threats to slaughter the Lord's disciples' (Acts 9:1). And, 'after he had spent only a few days with the disciples in Damascus, he began preaching in the synagogues, "Jesus is the Son of God" ' (Acts 9:20–1).

20

Whatever the changing molten convictions inside, they had to come out. Paul had to talk or burst. He talked his tireless way around the cities of the Graeco-Roman world, 'They addressed Barnabas as Zeus, and since Paul was the principal speaker they called him Hermes' (Acts 14:12). During the Diana riot at Ephesus he had to be almost physically restrained by the disciples from making a speech. Clearly the disciples thought it better to leave bad enough alone. Finally arrested in Jerusalem, and rescued by the Romans from the Jewish mob intent on his death, the prisoner probably astounded the arresting tribune by courteously asking for permission to make a speech. Paul especially liked to address a riot. More speeches during his captivity. In fact he was a sort of resident entertainer at the Roman camp in Caesarea, brought out to give a performance whenever distinguished visitors came along. I expect it never occurred to King Agrippa and Bernice, as, performance over, they returned to their evening banquet, that history would remember them at all only because they figured for a brief afternoon as audience to this vehement Jew, so much loved and hated, Roman citizen from Tarsus, Saul or Paul or whatever his name was. Prisoner aboard the storm-tossed ship heading precariously for Rome, Paul gives his fellow-travellers a sermonette about the God he serves, the angel who has appeared to him and the reassurance the angel had offered that all would be well. An improbable audience, and he must have seemed an improbable speaker as he gave this first Christian sermon-at-sea. He is presented as still talking when we bid him goodbye towards the end of Second Timothy; still saying what he had preached half a lifetime ago in Damascus, 'But the Lord stood by me and gave me power, so that through me the whole message might be proclaimed for all the pagans to hear' (II Timothy 4:17).

And yet, apparently, not a very gifted or impressive speaker. That is the impression from Paul's own words, 'Someone said, "He writes powerful and strongly worded letters, but when he is with you, you see only half a man and no preacher at all" ' (II Corinthians 10:10). He hints at the same mediocrity in his earlier Letter to Corinth, 'When I came to you, it was not with any show of oratory or philosophy but simply to tell you what God had guaranteed. . . . Far from relying on any power of my own, I came

21

among you in great "fear and trembling" ' (I Corinthians 2:1,3). Paul, tireless teacher and preacher; yet, apparently, he remained scared and nervous inside whenever he got up to speak.

And when he could not speak, he could write. His preaching was his apostolate to his own generation. His writings are his apostolate to the world. I do not want to delay here on Paul's mastery of language or his gifts as a writer. He can use all the tools: affectionate appeal, irony, sarcasm, denunciation, epigram, cogent argument, lyricism. Like any great writer, he can sometimes bore or irritate. But the greatness of his writing has little to do with his mastery of techniques. It has everything to do with a passionate personality; a man totally convinced, totally in love, meeting us on every page and sometimes in every paragraph. His writings are less exposition than invitation. Everywhere he keeps saying what he first said to the Corinthians, 'Take me for your model, as I take Christ' (I Corinthians 11:1). And there is more to it even than that. There is a unique and real Christ-presence in the Letters. If the whole corpus of Paul's Letters could speak, they might well say in almost the words of Paul, 'We live, now not we, but Christ lives in us.' That, I believe, is the real secret of their enduring charm. Through them Christ continues 'spreading the knowledge of himself, like a sweet smell, everywhere' (II Corinthians 2:14).

I have noted earlier Paul's closeness to and dependence on his friends. Nowhere does this come through so memorably as in the words attributed to Paul towards the end of the Second Letter to Timothy. The author, certainly an admirer of Paul and familiar with his Letters, is speaking out of a cherished tradition, if not from actual memory. He depicts Paul as an old man, the travels and battles nearly over, his mind constantly going back to the busy and golden days of apostolate 'and the persecutions and hardships that came to me in places like Antioch, Iconium and Lystra' (II Timothy 3:11).

Paul is depicted as old, lonely, most of his friends absent, Demas having deserted him for love of this world; only Luke is around. And he asks Timothy, almost begs Timothy, twice on one page, to come and to bring Mark with him before the winter begins. He is to bring the cloak, presumably a winter cloak, left with Carpus in Troas. Paul, no doubt, wants the warmth of this cloak about him

22

as the winter sets in. But far more than the cloak, he wants the warmth of his friends closely about him as a still longer winter comes near. 'Do your best to come before the winter' (II Timothy 4:21). This very human Paul needing his friends so badly is probably a good likeness. Was it weakness? Perhaps. And yet Christ also took care to gather his closest friends near about him the night before he died. It was partly of course because he loved them. But Christ needed them too.

It is worth while to dwell for a moment on the very first sample we get of Paul the missionary. The place is Paphos on the Island of Cyprus. The local Pro-Consul, Sergius Paulus, impressed by Barnabas and Saul, is thinking of becoming a Christian. A local Jewish magician called Bar Jesus is doing all he can to prevent Sergius from embracing Christianity,

> Then Saul, whose other name is Paul, looked him full in the face and said, 'You utter fraud, you imposter, you son of the devil, you enemy of all true religion, why don't you stop twisting the straightforward ways of the Lord? Now watch how the hand of the Lord will strike you: you will be blind and for a time you will not see the sun (Acts 13:9–11).

Nothing if not emphatic! Paul here reminds us of John the Baptist. And beyond John, of the great line of denunciatory prophets. The trenchant language of an Ezekiel or an Isaiah is a reminder how totally Paul was a Jew in the prophetic tradition. But the passage is even more revealing about the character of Paul.

Strong, impulsive, easily angered, vigorous and at times even savage in speech—that is how Paul the Apostle makes this, his grand entry, on the stage of apostolate. Sure of his truth and impatient of anyone or anything getting in the way. A man to whom criticism and opposition was goad not deterrent. An angry young man; well not exactly young, perhaps thirty-four. Paul's entry to apostolate, whatever else it was, was not particularly Christian. The outburst to Bar Jesus is hardly a striking illustration of what Paul would later enumerate as the fruits of the Spirit: charity, joy, peace, patience and the rest. It is encouraging to be reminded, right at the start of his great apostolate, of the Apostle's limitations. In more senses than one, Paul still had far to travel.

23

Chapter III

THE NEW WINE

Paul brought one lasting obsession to his entire apostolate. This was his conviction that Christianity must escape from the Jewish framework and categories in which it had been born. At the deepest level, of course, Paul saw Christianity as the fulfilment of Judaism, not its negation. But at a more superficial level there was the danger that Christianity might cling too closely to the trappings of Judaism and be strangled by them. It is hard for us to realise how urgent and desperately important this task of rescue seemed to Paul. It was literally a matter of life and death. If Christianity made the mistake of clinging to the Jewish womb which had borne it, it would certainly die.

The danger was real and unavoidable. Christian beginnings were steeped in Judaism. Christ, himself a Jew, had never lived or preached outside Palestine and its immediate borders. His personal mission was to the lost sheep of the house of Israel. In many ways he appeared to be just another itinerant Jewish teacher. True he spoke as no man spoke; he seemed endowed with unusual powers; he denounced the Pharisees, the Sadducees and the leaders of Judaism with vehemence. Still, all this was close enough to the tradition of the great prophets, the keepers of Israel's conscience against the dangers of ritualism, formalism and hypocrisy. Even Christ's closest friends, after the Resurrection and just before the Ascension, reveal an outlook still curiously limited by their Jewish assumptions, ' "Lord has the time come? Are you going to restore the kingdom to Israel?" ' (Acts 1:6.) After Christ's ascension, we find the Apostles 'continually in the temple praising God' (Luke 24:53). It is a revealing sentence. The Apostles still automatically

24

thought of the Jerusalem Temple as obviously the religious centre of the world. Peter himself, even after the enlightenment of Pentecost, needed a special vision from Heaven to drive him to the astonished, reluctant and for him revolutionary conclusion that the Christian message was for humanity, not just for the Jewish race, 'The truth I have now come to realise . . . is that God does not have favourites, but that anybody of any nationality who fears God and does what is right is acceptable to him' (Acts 10:34–5).

No favourites, any nationality—the texture of Peter's mind is clear. He had grown up in a tradition of a chosen favourite people. People of *any other* nationality were, at best, second-class citizens in God's kingdom. Peter still needed to shed this mentality. In charge of the new wine, he was nevertheless thinking automatically in terms of the old bottles. And if Peter was like this, how much more so the Judaeo-Christian community in Jerusalem. This community found it very difficult indeed to shed the Jewish swaddling clothes in which the Christian Church was wrapped from the beginning. Repeatedly, when we find Paul in contact with the church of Jerusalem, this smouldering question breaks into fresh flame. This, quite probably, was true even of Paul's first hurried visit to the church in Jerusalem—perhaps in AD 40. Naturally the Christians were cautious; could their persecutor be now really one of themselves? Anyhow, with hardly a pause he 'started to go around with them in Jerusalem preaching fearlessly in the name of the Lord' (Acts 9:28). There was a plot among the Hellenists to kill him and for that reason (or was it pretext?) the Apostles hustled him off to Tarsus, and Jerusalem for the moment was left in peace.

Reason or pretext? It is impossible to read the story closely without asking oneself the question. After all lots of Christians in or around Jerusalem were in danger. Why get so excited because one more Christian was on the run? And if the danger to Paul's life was only pretext what was the *reason* for getting him so quickly off the Jerusalem scene? It is a reasonable guess that Paul was a nuisance in Jerusalem because he was, or seemed, theologically dangerous. Paul might be safer out of Jerusalem; and Jerusalem (if the guess is right) felt much safer just then minus Paul. For, to this infant church, clinging desperately to all that could be retained of Jewish outlook and tradition, Paul must have seemed a disruptive

25

menace. Think for a moment of the frame of mind he must have brought with him after his encounter with the Risen Christ. There are three accounts of it—Acts, Chapters 9, 22 and 26. In the first of these Ananias was told, 'this man is my instrument to bring my name before pagans and pagan kings and [almost as an after-thought] before the people of Israel' (Acts 9:15). Already the last were beginning to be first and the first last. In a second version, Ananias is told that Paul is to be Christ's 'witness before all mankind' (Acts 22:15). No special favourites, no special place for Israel. In the final account the Risen Christ speaks of Paul's mission, not to Ananias, but directly to Paul himself, 'I shall deliver you from the people and from the pagans to whom I am sending you' (Acts 26:17). Throughout, the emphasis is on Paul's mission to mankind; there is not a hint of any need to tread warily or go slowly in order not to offend Jewish susceptibilities. The basics of this universalism Paul must have brought back with him from Damascus to Jerusalem. His ideas must have clashed violently with the more traditional ideas of many in the Christian community in Jerusalem. So very early in the Christian story do we find conflict about the never-quite-disappearing question: What does Christianity mean today? In our own time it is useful to reflect that a Church torn, almost torn apart, by the agony of efforts at fresh self-understanding would not appear to Paul an unfamiliar Church. Indeed with his arrival on the Jerusalem scene he would appear to have initiated the conflict.

Well known in Jerusalem, he was no doubt in greater danger there. But the Paul people remembered didn't run easily from danger, 'God's gift was not a spirit of timidity' (II Timothy 1:7). I find it difficult to believe that Paul would listen to arguments about *personal* risk. But the suggestion that his outlandish ideas were actually harming and even corrupting the Christian message—that would be another matter. Later on, in II Corinthians and Galatians, he gets furious with those who distort or corrupt Christ's message; so furious that you wonder if he is still smarting under a charge once made against himself. So I like to think of a rather lonely Paul, virtually rejected by the Christian community and its leaders, sadly leaving Jerusalem for Tarsus and knowing in his heart of hearts that many were breathing a sigh of relief at his going. If true, sad

26

and somewhat ironic. For more than any man on earth, more I imagine even than Peter, he carried with him in his heart a blurred but true vision of what Christianity was to be like in the world. It is one more illustration that loneliness is the mother country of the strong. No doubt he needed the bitter medicine of misunderstanding and rejection before he could adequately fulfil his destiny as Apostle to the Gentiles.

*

The question flared again when Peter came to Antioch possibly before, more probably after, the Council of Jerusalem.

> Cephas came to Antioch . . . When I saw they were not respecting the true meaning of the Good News, I said to Cephas in front of everyone, 'in spite of being a Jew, you live like the pagans and not like the Jews, so you have no right to make the pagans copy Jewish ways' (Galatians 2:11–14).

It is the one thing which consistently makes Paul angry: not respecting the true meaning of the Good News. Peter's reaction to this outburst is not recorded. At least it must have been abundantly clear to him that whatever else he had in Paul, he hadn't a 'yes man'. In passing, it is curious and regrettable how little emphasis one finds on courage in many a catalogue of Christian virtues. Among many kinds of necessary courage, that of plain speaking when plain speaking is necessary but may be unpopular is not the least. It is good to meet wherever you find it, whether in a Solzhenitsyin or a Paul. There is an old Gaelic proverb: *Taise le truagh agus; troid le traon*—with the weak be gentle; fight with the strong. The proverb would admirably fit Paul. He will be gentle as a mother with the runaway slave in the Letter to Philemon. But with Peter he won't mince or measure words.

*

The issue surfaced as the central question for the Council of Jerusalem. Let us glance first at the genesis of the Council.

Back in Antioch, the first missionary journey over, the big news Paul and Barnabas had was how God 'had opened the door of faith to the pagans' (Acts 14:27). But some visitors from the Church in Judea were less than enthusiastic. By now everybody, it appears, admitted that pagans *could* be admitted to the Christian community. The question was, what were they expected to do when let in? Should they be circumcised? It had long been the proud badge of God's people. Must they also observe the Mosaic Law? To both of these questions the Christians from Judea would answer Yes. Paul and Barnabas would offer an emphatic No. It was an inevitable disagreement about an unavoidable topic. It was, in fact, really part of a larger question: what was the relationship between the whole God-given Jewish tradition summed up as *the Law* and this new Way?

The argument in Antioch got nowhere. Yet it was too vital a question to sweep under the carpet. Luke tells us rather cryptically, '*it was arranged* that Paul and Barnabas and others of the Church should go up to Jerusalem and discuss the problem with the Apostles and the elders' (Acts 15:2).

'*It was arranged*'—the neutral phrase carefully avoids telling us who arranged it. Somebody must have suggested or pushed the idea. And surely all the evidence points to Paul or Barnabas and of these two more probably Paul who, quite clearly, had become the major partner in the combination. This was true ever since Antioch of Pisidia; up to then in Luke's story it is *Barnabas and Saul*, after that it is *Paul and Barnabas*. The stronger personality, the more gifted speaker, the more imaginative and more persuasive and in the long run probably the more clear sighted and determined on this vital issue, it was probably Paul, I suggest, who thought up and sold the idea of confronting the Apostles and elders in Jerusalem and having this matter out once for all. If so he was God's instrument, not merely for preaching the Gospel to the Gentiles, but also for summoning the first General Council of the Church. And, like most of the Councils, it was called not just to look calmly and dispassionately at Christian truth, but to deal with a crisis which might well have split the Church in two with Jerusalem and Antioch as the two centres of dissent. So often the route to fuller Christian truth lies along the path of sincere and emphatic disagreement.

28

'All the members of the church saw them off' (Acts 15:3)—so writes Luke of this departure of Paul and Barnabas from Antioch. There is no record of any other similar send-off in Acts. It reads rather like *all* the Ministers of a Cabinet, turning up at the airport to welcome home the Prime Minister if there is some sort of government crisis on. It was Antioch saying firmly to Jerusalem, 'This is Antioch's view and it's a strong one. You had better take it, and us, seriously.'

Jerusalem did. We are told that the discussion went on 'for a long time'. How long we do not know: We can only mournfully guess from our knowledge of Church history and our own experience. Peter's intervention seems to have been decisive in getting substantial acceptance for the Antioch point of view. Indeed, one gets the impression that Peter, anxious to lead in this area rather more adventurously than he could persuade his conservative community to follow, welcomed the opportunity to expose his local Christians to daring ideas of which they were afraid. You could sum up the first Ecumenical Council by saying that it was a triumph for Paul's ideas but in some ways a personal disappointment and even humiliation for Paul.

For what was Paul's claim as we find it in his letters? As good an example as any other is the opening of the Letter to the Galatians, 'From Paul . . . an apostle who does not owe his authority to men or his appointment to any human being but who has been appointed by Jesus Christ and by God the Father who raised Jesus from the dead' (Galatians 1:1). His claim is that, just as much as Peter, James, John or the others, he has been personally called to be an Apostle by Christ. How did that claim fare at the Council of Jerusalem?

It was ignored. Take Peter's speech, 'My brothers you know perfectly well that . . . the pagans were to learn the Good News from *me* and so become believers' (Acts 15:7). Not a word about Paul who claimed this as *his* special mission and who, listening to Peter, must have reflected that he had preached to hundreds of pagans while Peter would probably have counted them in tens or twenties. And Paul, making the claim he did, must have been disappointed and deeply hurt by the phrase used in the letter about dietary laws sent about this time by James to the Gentiles in Anti-

29

och, Syria and Cilicia, 'Barnabas and Paul, men we highly respect, who have dedicated their lives to the name of our Lord Jesus Christ' (Acts 15:26). The phrase is remarkable not so much for what it says as what it fails to say. No reference to Paul as the Apostle of the Gentiles. No reference to his work and that of Barnabas among the pagans from Antioch to Lystra. No reference to the understanding, described by Paul in Galatians, that Paul had been sent by God to the pagans, Peter to the circumcised. Paul (the clear implication of the Letter runs) is a good Christian and a zealous worker for Christianity. Yes. But as for being one of *us*, one of the Apostles, well the less said about that the better. Let's drop the topic and it, and he, will go away.

Paul emerges in his letters as a man who desperately needed human acceptance and encouragement. For most of his apostolic life a very heavy part of the cross he had to bear was that of being misunderstood and not fully accepted by those who had walked closest to the Lord. It must have been with the familiar human mixture of elation and deep dejection that Paul, after the first Council, made his way back, I almost said made his way home, from Jerusalem to Antioch. I expect Antioch was as near as Paul had to a home once he began to preach the Gospel. Like Cain, he had become a fugitive and a wanderer over the earth.

Not that Paul remained entirely consistent about circumcision. We actually find him having Timothy circumcised 'on account of the Jews in the locality' (Acts 16:3). And he is again ambivalent, to put it mildly, when the Christian leaders in Jerusalem ask for a public indication that 'there is no truth in the reports that they have heard about you and that you still regularly observe the Law' (Acts 21:24). Had Paul weakened or had he mellowed? Or did he, perhaps, feel towards the end of his days in Asia that, the main battle won, he could afford to make irenic gestures? One doubts if anybody can be sure.

*

All this controversy gives us the flavour of the times and highlights a serious danger confronting the early Church. If leaders like Peter and James could slip back so easily into Jewish ways, how much greater the danger must have been for the run-of-the-mill Jewish convert! From there it was only a short step to imposing circumcision and all that went with it on Gentile converts as well, so making circumcision the hallmark also of Christianity. Against this danger Paul guarded the bridge proclaiming to all what he wrote to the Galatians, 'In Christ Jesus, whether you are circumcised or not makes no difference—what matters is the faith that makes its power felt through love' (Galatians 5:6). The most serious threat to Christianity, in Paul's view, was not from Gentiles who would reject, oppose or persecute it. The real danger came from within, from Jewish converts who would misunderstand and distort the Good News of Jesus Christ by recasting it in the moulds of Judaism, so destroying the universal character of Christianity.

Paul found recidivism almost everywhere: a tendency to lapse back into Jewish ways and assumptions. He saw traces of it in Barnabas and James and even in Cephas. So be it: he would continue to trumpet the truth. I believe this is the key to one of the many paradoxes we find in Paul. He tells us again and again how much he loves his own people; and yet there is hardly a Letter in which he does not denounce those of the circumcision. He could see all the privileges and glories of the Old Testament as introduction to Christ; never as alternative to Christ. Converts from Judaism, he insisted, could be faithful to their proud traditions only in transcending them. Lines that Goldsmith wrote about Edmund Burke sum it up:

Who, born for the universe, narrowed his mind
And gave up to party what was meant for mankind.

Christianity, born for the universe, must be kept for mankind. It fell to Paul, more than any other man, to rescue Christianity from the danger of being smothered by its swaddling clothes of Judaism. He saw this as an exceedingly important part of his vocation. It is useful reminder how the precise agenda of an apostle in any age are largely determined by the needs of that age; and it is also useful warning against a monochrome apostolate.

When Paul, then, denounces Judaism and the Judaisers, in the long run he is not denouncing but defending. Defending what? The

31

universality of the Christian message, at its heart the universa
Christ we meet in Colossians or Ephesians.

PART TWO

Paul And Prayer

Chapter IV

'BEHOLD HE IS PRAYING'
(Acts 9:11.)

Thus far the emphasis has been on travel, tumult and controversy. It is high time to turn to Paul and prayer.

Writing to his Corinthian converts about AD 57, Paul uses a much-quoted phrase, 'Though this outer man of ours may be falling into decay, the inner man is renewed day by day' (II Corinthians 4:16). Whatever the precise meaning Paul originally attached to the words *outer man* and *inner man*, they can be used as a rough description of the Acts of the Apostles as opposed to the Pauline Letters. Acts, on the whole, gives the man of travel and action, of riots and controversy, the outer man. The Letters give us more of the mind and heart of Paul. Providence made sure to give us a full picture, Acts and the Letters complementing each other.

Not that the Acts are exclusively outer man or the Letters exclusively inner man. The Letters tell us quite a lot about Paul's travels and problems that we wouldn't know from Acts. Conversely Acts gives us many rich glimpses of what Paul most deeply was as well as what he did. This is particularly true of what I may call, for want of a better name, Paul's prayer life. Even if we had only Acts, and no Letters, Paul would emerge indisputably as a man whose life was steeped in prayer. Just now I look at the *fact* of Paul's prayer life rather than at its intimate texture. I begin by looking at whatever evidence there is in Acts.

Paul doesn't appear in Acts until Chapter 8 and doesn't come to stay until Chapter 9. To get this matter of Paul and prayer into perspective, it is useful to recall how, before the advent of Paul, the

35

young Christian community was already very much a community of prayer. Like Paul himself, the community sprang out of a rich Jewish tradition of prayer. The synagogue, the centre of Jewish religious life, was primarily a house of prayer and in a special way this was true of the Temple in Jerusalem. The Moslem custom of turning towards Mecca for prayer is said to be a derivative of a Jewish tradition when Jews found themselves far away from the Temple. So it is not surprising that the early Christian community repeatedly emerges in the first eight chapters of Acts as very much a praying community.

In Chapter 1, for example, we read that the Apostles, just after the Ascension, 'joined in continuous prayer . . . with . . : Mary the mother of Jesus' (Acts 1:14). The whole assembly prayed before the selection of Matthias in the same chapter. At the end of Chapter 2 a phrase summing up the community life says, 'These remained faithful to the teaching of the Apostles, to the brotherhood, to the breaking of the bread and to the prayers' (Acts 2:42). The beginning of Chapter 3 shows us Peter and John going up to the Temple 'for the prayers at the ninth hour' (Acts 3:1). After the release of Peter and John in Chapter 4, the Christian group 'lifted up their voice to God all together' (Acts 4:24). Chapter 5 has no reference to prayer but at the beginning of Chapter 6, when the Apostles decide to institute deacons, the stated purpose is that the Apostles should 'continue to devote ourselves to prayer and to the service of the Word' (Acts 6:4). When the chosen deacons were presented to the Apostles, the twelve 'prayed and laid their hands on them' (Acts 6:6). At the end of Chapter 7 Stephen, being stoned to death, cries out in prayer, 'Lord Jesus receive my spirit' (Acts 7:59), and then, in this matter Christ's first imitator, goes on to pray for those putting him to death. At the end of life, as at the beginning of ministry, prayer came almost as naturally as breathing. Prayer was prayer for all times.

I glance at one further interesting example of the place of prayer among the early Christians. Peter and John, visiting some converts in Samaria, found that these, although baptised, had not received the Holy Spirit. The two Apostles 'prayed for the Samaritans to receive the Holy Spirit' (Acts 8:15). It brings one back to Luke's Gospel where Christ, talking about the invariable efficacy of prayer, says, 'If you then, who are evil, know how to give your children what is good, how much more will the Heavenly Father give the Holy Spirit to those who ask him' (Luke 11:13). It would appear that, in the vision of Christ this gift of the Holy Spirit is the only gift really worth asking for or worth giving. It is a profound topic to which I hope to return.

Well before Paul, then, the Christian community, emerging as it did from a Spirit-guided Jewish tradition, was a community of prayer. Indeed, was this the chief fruit of God's Spirit, hovering over the waters at the beginning and, across the unfolding centuries, especially moulding the destinies of the Jewish people? In the Pauline vision the chief and immediate fruit of the descent of the Holy Spirit into a soul is to enable and impel that soul to say, 'Abba Father.' Perhaps this is as good a way as any other to see the story of Israel from Abraham to Mary: the slow preparation by the Spirit of a people's prayer so that it could be ready, in some measure, to understand, receive and even echo the new level of prayer to come with Christ and in which we have been invited to participate when Christ taught us the Our Father. If so, the chief journey of the people of Israel was a journey in prayer across a frightening and sometimes barren wilderness of unbelief and infidelity. In this vision the Psalms become central: the halting articulations of something that will become perfect only on the lips of Christ. It is interesting that Luke puts on the lips of the risen Christ a reference to 'everything written about me . . . in the Psalms' (Luke 24:44). In a sense, the Psalms were the choir practice of the race in preparation for the hymn of the universe that would be sung by Christ. And we find in the Canticles attributed to Zachary and Mary by Luke the final and fitting overtures of the Spirit-guided human orchestra before the coming-on-stage of the great singer and his song.

Practically the first thing we hear about Paul, the convert, is (in the words of our Lord to Ananias), 'At this moment he is praying' (Acts 9:11). So his life as a Christian began. So it continued. A glance here and there in Acts gives us some idea of the atmosphere of prayer in which Paul lived, moved and had his being.

The atmosphere emerges clearly when Paul is set apart by the Holy Spirit for his mission to the Gentiles. The call came when the Christian community in Antioch was 'offering worship to the Lord and keeping a fast' (Acts 13:2), thus placing the greatest apostolic vocation of all time in a setting of penance and prayer. 'After fasting and prayer' (Acts 13:3) the local Church laid hands on Barnabas and Paul and sent them off; it was the first missionary departure. A few chapters later we find Paul and Silas in Philippi, 'we went along the river outside the gates as it was the sabbath and this was a customary place for prayer' (Acts 16:12). The place of prayer attracted Paul as the light attracts the moth. Still in Philippi, after Paul and Silas had been scourged, they were thrown into an inner prison with their feet in the stocks. Hardly comfortable, and we could expect Paul and Silas to relax to the very limited extent that circumstances permitted. But, Luke tells us, 'Late that night Paul and Silas were praying and singing God's praises while other prisoners listened' (Acts 16:25). Paul and Silas were probably lucky to be in the *inner* prison that night! One can easily imagine the reaction of other prisoners being deprived of their sleep by these two strange characters who kept chanting away mysteriously at the top of their voices and praying at that!

It is in the discourse attributed to Paul at Athens that we get the first glimpse in Acts of the *texture* of Paul's prayer. It is only a glimpse, but a precious one, for here he is presented as desperately trying to explain to a group of sceptics how he conceives of this deity he has crossed half the Roman world to preach. Not a remote deity, 'He is not far from any of us since it is in him that we . . . move and exist' (Acts 17:27). Not a God uninterested in the human adventure, 'He decreed how long each nation should flourish and what the boundaries of its territory should be' (Acts 17:26). A God who wants to be sought and found by men: he has guided history so that 'all nations might seek the deity and by feeling their way towards him, succeed in finding him' (Acts 17:27). All, of course, leading to the great central affirmation, which probably meant nothing to his listeners but meant almost everything to Paul, 'Since we are the children of God . . .' (Acts 17:29). How much it ultimately meant to Paul we can learn from the Letter to the Ephesians even though this, as many of the scholars tell us, may be the work of a disciple rather than being strictly speaking a letter written or dictated by Paul. But we have the root in Athens of what will be full flower in Ephesians. Incredible sonship of God in Jesus Christ is the core of Pauline thought and the ultimate basis of Pauline prayer.

Paul's stop-off at Miletus (Acts 20:17) to say a last good-bye to his chief helpers from Ephesus is one of the most moving passages in Acts. In his talk (Lucan composition but rich in Pauline echoes) to them he first looks back nostalgically at all they and he have done and been through together. He also looks forward to a future which, for himself, contains, obscurely, imprisonment and persecution; a future for them of problems, difficulties, heresies, schisms, persecution. At the centre of that past and that future he put, of course, 'the Lord Jesus who himself said, "There is more happiness in giving than in receiving" ' (Acts 20:35). For Paul there is never any other centre. Finally all has been said that can be said and there is no more that human interchange of words can do. There is only prayer.

> So he knelt down with them all and prayed. By now they were all in tears: they put their arms around Paul's neck and kissed him; what saddened them most was his saying that they would never see his face again (Acts 20:36–8).

It reminds me of the Last Supper; for Christ, too, at the end there was only prayer for and with his own. 'When we had at last torn ourselves away from them' (Acts 21:1)—that is the phrase Luke uses to describe the departure from Miletus. We can hardly miss here the clear picture of a man who both gave and received treasures of affection.

I have looked at various passages from Acts where we find Paul engaged in *ordinary* prayer, prayer within the reach of any committed Christian. But the picture would be incomplete if we did not recognise in Paul's life also the element of *extraordinary* prayer, the visions, the revelations and the rest. It began at Damascus. To meet the Risen Christ; to be addressed by him by personal name in what turns out to be complaint and commission is no ordinary beginning in a Christian life. That this special destiny keeps breaking in we are repeatedly reminded by Acts. Apart from the Damascus experience, the reference to these divine interventions is always scanty and fleeting. Nevertheless a glance at them may help us to understand Paul's inner life and indeed also his whirlwind activity a shade better.

It seems probable that the vision of Christ recorded in Acts, Chapter 22 was the first vision after Damascus.

> Once, after I had got back to Jerusalem, when I was praying in the Temple, I fell into a trance and then I saw him. 'Hurry,' he said, 'leave Jerusalem at once; they will not accept the testimony you are giving about me.' 'Lord', I answered, 'it is because they know that I used to go from synagogue to synagogue, imprisoning and flogging those who believed in you; and that when the blood of your witness Stephen was being shed, I was standing by in full agreement with his murderers, and minding their clothes.' Then he said to me, 'Go! I am sending you out to the pagans far away' (Acts 22:17–21).

There are a number of interesting things about this story. First of all there is the taken-for-granted, no-eyebrows-raised fact that Paul prayed *in the Temple*, clinging in spite of everything to the sacred centre of Jewish worship. It reminds us that Paul saw Christianity as continuity in addition to seeing it as a new creation. Second, there is the fact that Christ chose to appear *there* of all places. But it is of a piece with his lament over Jerusalem. Christ must have loved Jerusalem and its Temple very much indeed in spite of a rent veil. But even more interesting is the picture of Paul still struggling against his vocation, like Jacob wrestling with God. Even though he had been clearly told about his special call to the Gentiles, he is anxious to be about another work: to preach to the Jews in and around Jerusalem. But his past rises up like a ghost against him, nobody will listen and Paul in despair is praying in the Temple, praying against what God means him to be. From the tense phrases of Acts, I imagine him as in tears. But there is no escape. Christ's words are brief and almost brusque: 'Hurry, leave Jerusalem at once . . . Go! I am sending you out to the pagans far away' (Acts 22:18–21). At Damascus Paul had asked Christ two questions. The second one was, 'What do you wish me to do?' Now Paul hears finally, fully and inescapably Christ's pitiless answer, sending him to the impossible. Or rather sending him on a journey along which he would later cry out in astonished gratitude, 'There

40

is nothing I cannot master with the help of the One who gives me strength' (Philippians 4:13).

This Temple vision told Paul in broad terms what he had to do. The next recorded divine intervention is, by contrast, intriguingly specific. It tells Paul precisely where to go or rather where not to go. Paul was thinking of going to the Roman province of Asia until 'told by the Holy Spirit not to preach the word in Asia' (Acts 16:6). He next thought of Bithynia 'but the Spirit of Jesus would not allow them' (Acts 16:7). Soon, in Troas came the vision of a Macedonian pleading: 'Come across to Macedonia and help us' (Acts 16:9). All this raises the question to what extent Paul's journeys were dictated in some detail by the Holy Spirit.

If we had only these passages we might be tempted to think, somewhat enviously, of Paul's life as signposted in detail by signs from Heaven. But this would be false to the total picture which shows us in the main a Paul having to make his own decisions but more strikingly guided just now and then at turning points of decisive importance. Put into to-day's terms, Paul had mostly to decide his own priorities and make hard decisions. It should be encouraging to missionaries of all time that Paul, too, had problems of decisions; had to be guided by his fallible human judgement. A good example of Paul in perplexity is found in Galatians: 'I must go through the pain of giving birth to you all over again until Christ is formed in you. I wish I were with you now so that I could know exactly what to say; as it is, I have no idea what to do for the best' (Galatians 4:19).

The last sentence or something like it is often in the heart of many an apostle.

But even if the human perplexity is inescapable, it should also be encouraging to reflect how closely and constantly the Holy Spirit hovered over Paul's wayfaring, intervening in an obvious way only when Paul was about to take a dangerous step; rather like a mother watching over her child learning to walk but mostly letting him do it on his own. Perhaps we do not sufficiently remember in our perplexities Christ's promise of a Spirit who would guide us into all truth. If we did remember, perhaps we would talk less and listen more. And learn something in the process about the source and size of Christian courage.

Christian courage! Paul had more need of it than most, and courage is the dominating theme in the remaining three Pauline visions. At Corinth Christ appeared to Paul and told him, 'Do not be afraid to speak out, nor allow yourself to be silenced' (Acts 18:9). The day after Paul's arrest in Jerusalem Christ appeared to him in the Roman fortress, 'Courage, you have borne witness for me in Jerusalem, now you must do the same in Rome' (Acts 23:11). And in the final vision, this time aboard the Rome-bound ship, we find Paul telling his frightened fellow-travellers, 'Last night there was standing beside me an angel of the God to whom I belong and whom I serve, and he said "Do not be afraid, Paul" ' (Acts 27:23). Does this emphasis on courage tell us something important about Paul? Our Lord hardly gives superfluous or irrelevant advice; yet three times we find him exhorting Paul to courage. Was this perhaps Paul's abiding temptation—often the temptation of the Christian—to lose heart, to get tired and fed up with it all? Writing to the Corinthians we find Paul so overcome by it all that in his own words, 'the things we had to undergo in Asia were more of a burden than we could carry, so that we despaired of coming through alive' (II Corinthians 1:8). His mood of discouragement is impossible to miss; life as an Apostle was getting him badly down. If a Paul could feel like that, how easy it is to understand a similar frame of mind in many a Christian up against it to-day! Karl Rahner has a phrase somewhere about the everyday dust settling remorselessly down on everything. He is speaking of priestly ministry and what he says is profoundly true of apostolate even at its best. But at its worst—compounded perhaps by uncongenial companionship, failing health and apparent failure—it can certainly demand the kind of desperate courage to which the Lord kept urging St Paul in his moments of blackness and near despair.

All of which makes one wonder about the 'thorn in the flesh' in the twelfth chapter of II Corinthians. The thorn may have been a physical defect (perhaps eye trouble) or temptation against chastity or any other of the various possibilities which have been suggested. But Our Lord's repeated exhortation to courage makes me wonder whether the thorn in the flesh may not have been a neurotic, perhaps near-psychotic tendency in Paul to depression. In the passage from II Corinthians just referred to, Paul talks of 'the agonies I go through for Christ's sake' (II Corinthians 12:10). Anybody who has ever talked to a priest going through a bad depression period will know how agonising and paralysing these agonies can be. Indeed the whole of this Second Letter to the Corinthians breathes the mixture of acute depression and high elation typical of the man who lives on his nerves and frequently gets on those of other people. His psychiatrist, if Paul had had one, would probably have prescribed tranquillisers. If all this was part of Paul's problem, it makes him in a special way the patron of not a few, in the ministry and outside it, today. How much suffering this temperament brings, only those cursed or blessed with it fully understand. But it should be reassuring for those with this temperament to recall Christ's words to Paul when the latter begged repeatedly that his thorn in the flesh should be taken away, 'My grace is enough for you: my power is at its best in weakness.' Reassuring, too, is Paul's reaction, 'I shall be very happy to make my weaknesses my special boast so that the power of Christ may stay over me . . . for it is when I am weak that I am strong' (II Corinthians 12:9–10). Perhaps this was centrally what St Paul was talking about when he wrote to the Colossians about his wish to fill up in his own body what was still wanting in the sufferings of Christ. After all, the Agony in the Garden was chiefly an agony in the mind.

Some years ago in Toledo, the home of El Greco which still possesses many of his masterpieces, I was looking at his famous pictures of the twelve Apostles. A guide to the museum told me a story about El Greco which I had never heard before. The artist, when asked to paint the Apostles, did a curious thing. He went off to the local lunatic asylum and looked over the inmates there. He chose twelve of them as his models and (so the guide assured me) one can still see the authorisation granted for this by those then in charge of the institution. After hearing this story, I found myself looking at the Apostles, specially at their eyes, with a new understanding. Call it vision in their eyes or call it some hint of madness, there was more there than the light of common day. Chesterton once wrote of Irishmen:

For the great Gaels of Ireland
Are men whom God made mad.

43

Maybe the lines have also some relevance to apostolate and apostles. Kierkegaard wrote somewhere that Christianity is fire and Christians are incendiaries. If you were looking around for an incendiary you would hardly search among people eminently sensible, settled and sedate. It looks as if God thought rather along the same lines when he was looking around for a man who would set the world on fire. Paul got the job.

Chapter V

'PRAY ALL THE TIME'
(EPHESIANS 6:18)

I have looked at some of the evidence in Acts that Paul lived in a
continual atmosphere of prayer. I now turn to his Letters. These,
even more than Acts, bring it home how, for Paul, prayer was part
of his being as much as breathing. Take it away and you just
wouldn't have the Paul we know.

When we write a letter today we put it in an envelope. I don't
know what Paul wrapped up his letters in. Presumably he must
have wrapped them up in something. But there is always one
invariable wrapping. All Paul's letters are wrapped up in prayer.
I take one or two examples of the wrappings, the first from a Letter
to a church Paul did not personally know at all, the church at
Rome:

> First I thank my God through Jesus Christ for all of you and the way
> in which your faith is spoken of all over the world. The God I worship
> spiritually by preaching the Good News of his Son knows that I never
> fail to mention you in my prayers (Romans 1:8).

Sixteen chapters, many splendours and much obscurity later,
Paul, having said all he wanted to say (and Tertius the scribe, no
doubt, saying a private fervent *Deo gratias*) turns again to prayer:

> Glory to Him who is able to give you the strength to live according to
> the Good News I preach, and in which I proclaim Jesus Christ ... it
> is all part of the way the eternal God wants things to be. He alone is
> wisdom; give glory therefore to him through Jesus Christ for ever and
> ever. Amen (Romans 16:25–7).

I think Paul would have found almost unintelligible a catechesis that didn't spring from prayer and find its climax in prayer. Romans is probably the greatest story ever told about the mercy of God and the need of man. Theologians from Augustine to Karl Barth have struggled with its deeps. For Paul, the whole profound meditation would be pointless unless it were a prelude to prayer and praise.

A second illustration of how Paul's Letters are wrapped up in prayer I take, by contrast, from a Letter to a church he knew perhaps better than any other, his wayward, backsliding, infuriating, occasionally penitent and always much beloved Corinthians. Either of his Letters to Corinth would provide a good illustration but I choose II Corinthians because I am particularly fond of it. This Letter teaches us at least as much as any other Pauline Letter about the human Paul. Here he wears his heart on his sleeve; it is a very tattered sleeve and a tormented heart. It is a good Letter to read and reread when things have gone wrong and there is a temptation to be discouraged, despairing or even bitter about the reality of ministry and apostolate.

Paul has hardly begun this Second Letter to the Corinthians when we find him in grateful, suffering, confident prayer:

Blessed be the God and Father of our Lord Jesus Christ, a gentle Father and the God of all consolation, who comforts us in all our sorrows, so that we can offer others, in their sorrows, the consolation that we have received from God ourselves. Indeed as the sufferings of Christ overflow to us, so through Christ, does our consolation overflow (II Corinthians 1:3–5).

The first thing I should like to note about this prayer is how it begins on a note of gratitude and praise. An initial expression of gratitude was, of course, commonplace in letter-writing in the time of Paul. On this practice Paul, in his letters, builds his prayer of thanks and praise. Gratitude for his Christians is one of the outstanding elements of Pauline prayer. How very often we find Paul thanking God for his converts and for all the graces God has poured out on them! This is true of early Paul, late Paul and middle Paul. Take the first of his Letters, I Thessalonians, 'We always mention you in our prayers and thank God for you all' (1:3). Similarly II

Thessalonians opens on the note of gratitude, 'We feel we must be continually thanking God for you, brothers' (1:3). The introduction to Romans we have already looked at; it, too, is gratitude and praise. The same note is evident at the beginning of I Corinthians, 'I never stop thanking God for all the graces you have received through Jesus Christ. I thank him that you have been enriched in so many ways especially in your preachers and teachers' (1:4). Philippians is the same: 'I thank my God whenever I think of you; and every time I pray for all of you, I pray with joy' (1:3). Colossians is no different: 'We have never failed to remember you in our prayers and to give thanks for you to God, the Father of our Lord Jesus Christ' (1:3). The recurring emphasis is unmistakable. Whenever Paul thinks of his scattered converts, and he was by no means blind to their shortcomings, his first impulse is to break into *Magnificat* for the children who may have ten thousand schoolmasters in Christ but only one Father.

This Pauline trait is less than obtrusive in our pastoral spirituality today! The people God gives us figure, no doubt, in our prayers, but are they there more as objects of petition than sources of gratitude? Paul's concern for his people always led him, of course, to pray for their needs but normally only after a cry of gratitude for them and all that God had given them. Maybe, while still needing petition for our people, we could do with more of *Magnificat*. Inside my own church, it does not dominate the Bidding Prayers of the Mass.

The prayer that closes II Corinthians is, happily, now often on our lips. It is one of the simplest and most beautiful of Pauline Prayers, 'The grace of the Lord Jesus Christ, the love of God and the fellowship of the Holy Spirit be with you all' (II Corinthians 13:13).

Could any Christian ask for more in this life? Or for that matter in the life to come?

*

So much for the setting of the Pauline epistles, normally set between two poles of prayer. Also enlightening are the many passages in the Letters where Paul insistently urges his converts to a life of prayer.

47

These give us some idea what Paul expected from his Christian communities and, beyond that, give us undoubtedly a picture of Paul's own practice. Paul was not a man to preach one thing and do another. The first passage I look at is from Colossians:

> With gratitude in your hearts sing psalms and hymns and inspired songs to God; and never say or do anything except in the name of the Lord Jesus, giving thanks to God the Father through him (Colossians 3:16–17).

Gratitude again! On Paul's gratitude for his Christian people I have already dwelt. But this is only part of a wider and richer landscape of gratitude. Indeed if I had to choose the outstanding theme of all Pauline prayer, gratitude is the theme I would choose: his spontaneous prayer is *Magnificat*. There is gratitude for his deliverance from the inner turmoil and frustration he had experienced during his efforts to live by the Law, 'What a wretched man I am. Who will rescue me from this body doomed to death? Thanks be to God through Jesus Christ, our Lord' (Romans 7:24). There is gratitude for God's closeness in the dull daily grind of apostolate, 'Thanks be to God who, wherever he goes, makes us, in Christ, partners of his triumph, and through us is spreading the knowledge of himself, like a sweet smell, everywhere' (II Corinthians 2:14). For Paul, all is gift; therefore all is thanks.

> It is by grace that you have been saved, through faith; not by anything of your own, but by a gift from God; not by anything that you have done, so that nobody can claim the credit. We are God's work of art, created in Christ Jesus (Ephesians 2:8–10).

In Colossians he visualises his Christians as always 'thanking the Father who has made it possible for you to join the saints and with them to inherit the light' (Colossians 1:12). Whether we think of his example or his instruction, for Paul, the Christian life is constant Eucharist, always giving thanks. This emphasis is especially clear in a familiar passage from Ephesians.

> Do not drug yourselves with wine, this is simply dissipation; be filled with the Spirit. Sing the words and tunes of the psalms and hymns

48

when you are together, and go on singing to the Lord in your hearts, so that always and everywhere you are giving thanks to God who is our Father in the name of our Lord Jesus Christ (Ephesians 5:18–20).

'*Always and everywhere . . . giving thanks to God . . .*' Once again one notes the central place of constant joyful gratitude. In this passage Paul seems to think of the community meeting, with its words, tunes, hymns and psalms as the central focus of Christian prayer; presumably this was centred around the Eucharist. But it is a focus that is to overflow and, after the meeting, they are to go on singing and chanting gratefully to the Lord in their hearts, always and everywhere. It has a curiously contemporary ring. Vatican II is presenting much the same truth when it tells us that the Eucharist is to be the source and centre of our Christian lives, certainly, therefore, the source and centre of our prayer. The emphasis is contemporary but the truth emphasised is as old as Paul. 'Pray all the time, asking for what you need, praying in the Spirit on every possible occasion' (Ephesians 6:18). Here too, as in the previous chapter (5:18), Paul associates closely the *Spirit* with Christian prayer. He tells them to '*be filled with the Spirit*' and then spells out what this will mean—a life of continuous and grateful prayer. '*Praying in the Spirit on every possible occasion*'—it reminds us how for Paul, prayer and the Spirit-filled life are practically synonymous. Sonship, Spirit, prayer—this trinity is never far from Paul's thoughts.

*

Paul's prayer of thanksgiving for his people was steeped in joy. There is no point in repeating texts to underline something so inescapable. One text from Philippians sums up this aspect of Paul's prayer, 'Every time I pray for all of you I pray with joy' (Philippians 1:5). He wrote it to Philippi but he could have written it just as well to Corinth or Galatia or Ephesus. Towards the end of Philippians he talks intimately of his deepest wishes for them, 'I want you to be happy, happy in the Lord; I repeat, what I want is your happiness' (Philippians 4:4). We of a later and less exultant Christianity might, in similar circumstances, have written: 'What I want is your holiness.' But Paul wrote happiness, not holiness. Appar-

49

ently he did not see much difference between the two.

Gratitude, gladness—and also growth. For Paul, Christianity is splendid new birth. But, just as on the physical level, Christian birth is only the beginning, and the child of God is born to grow. We constantly find him imploring the Father that these new feeble children may grow; especially that they may grow in faith, hope and love. Paul is constant practitioner of the prayer of petition. But he never trivialises the prayer of petition. His converts had the daily problems of people everywhere: illnesses, marital problems, worries about the children. No doubt he encouraged his converts to bring these familiar daily needs to their loving Father. All that, one feels sure, is part of what he had in mind when he wrote to Philippi,

> There is no need to worry; but if there is anything you need, pray for it, asking God for it with prayer and thanksgiving, and that peace of God, which is so much greater than we can understand, will guard your hearts and your thoughts in Christ Jesus (Philippians 4:7).

Even here, when Paul is encouraging his Christians to pray for their everyday needs, he gives no assurance that their specific requests will be granted. He seems far more concerned with, and sure about, the peace of God greater than our understanding which will come to them through trusting prayer. And when he prays for his converts, invariably he follows the rule he laid down for the Corinthians, 'Be ambitious for the higher gifts' (I Corinthians 12:31). Paul, pleading for his people, asks not for the trivial or the fleeting in life but the higher gifts. 'We pray continually that our God will make you worthy of his call, and by his power fulfil all your desires for goodness and complete all that you have been doing through faith' (II Thessalonians 1:11). His mind is on the same abiding values when he prays for his Christians in Philippi, 'My prayer is that your love for each other may increase more and more and never stop improving your knowledge and deepening your perception so that you can always recognise what is best' (Philippians 1:9). It is the same in Colossians, 'What we ask God is that through perfect wisdom and spiritual understanding you should reach the fullest knowledge of his will' (Colossians 1:9). In Ephesians, uniquely the Letter of prayer, Paul intersperses his praises of

God with petition for his people. 'May the God of our Lord Jesus Christ, the Father of glory, give you a spirit of wisdom and perception of what is revealed, to bring you to full knowledge of him. May he enlighten the eyes of your mind' (Ephesians 1:17–18). Finally there is the familiar prayer of Chapter 3 of Ephesians—in which he asks that Christ may live in their hearts through faith, that they may be rooted and founded in love, that they may fathom Christ's love beyond all knowledge and so be filled with the utter fullness of God. Paul cares too much for his Christians to pray for the transient or the trivial. He wants only the best for his children.

Paul, then, praying for his people, never asks for the trivial and seems slow to ask for the specific. This may well be because he had discovered, from personal experience, that God, in his unfailing response to prayer, grants what he chooses, not necessarily what we ask. We have just one case of Paul asking for a specific favour for himself, 'I was given a thorn in the flesh . . . I have pleaded with the Lord three times for it to leave me' (II Corinthians 12:7–8). God refused the specific request, but heard the prayer by making this weakness of Paul, whatever it was, the occasion for growth in dependence on Christ. Paul's prayer here is curiously reminiscent of a prayer in the Garden also repeated three times; that request was denied but the prayer was heard. The experience of Christ and Paul suggests that our prayers of petition are more important in that they express our dependence and joyful trust than in any assurance that our Father will give us precisely the things we ask for, 'Your Father knows what you need before you ask him' (Matthew 6:8). Knows what you really need, not what you think you need. It would be a very unloving father, and not the Christian God, were he to listen to our prattlings about our imaginary needs instead of supplying needs that are deep and real.

*

Still on the subject of Paul urging prayer, there are at least three occasions in his Letters where he explicitly asks his Christians for *their* prayers for the success of his apostolate—II Corinthians 1:11, Ephesians 6:19, and Colossians 4:3. I draw attention to a point emerging from the passages in Ephesians and Colossians:

51

> Pray for us specially, asking God to show us opportunities for announcing the message and proclaiming the mystery of Christ for the sake of which I am in chains; pray that I may proclaim it as clearly as I ought (Colossians 4:3).

> Pray for me to be given an opportunity to open my mouth and speak without fear . . . pray that in proclaiming it I may speak as boldly as I ought to (Ephesians 6:19).

Paul, presumably, sought prayers for what he felt specially in need of: courage in apostolate. The practice of asking people to pray for our apostolic work has clearly a very respectable ancestry. Sometimes today in books or essays on prayer one finds an explanation of petitionary prayer that is in reality an apology for petitionary prayer. The explanations can end by explaining it away. The trouble with this is that it is entirely against the practice of Paul and the teaching of Christ. Petitionary prayer does not dominate Paul's concept or practice of prayer but it is certainly there and it looms large. Paul is as good a guide as we are likely to find. He did, after all, claim to have in quite a special way the mind of Christ.

*

Paul preached a Christian life always only a diaphanous veil away from a background of prayer and praise. His Letters reveal a man who, at the drop of a thought, slips almost unconsciously from prose into prayer. The Letters abound with examples. I look at a few, the first from Romans.

During eight intricate and closely argued chapters, Paul has been considering how God's mercy gratuitously reaches sinful man; from the beginning of Chapter 9 onwards he has been looking at God's mercy as it uniquely reaches the Jewish people. Paul is overcome by this vast panorama of mercy and, by a sort of spontaneous combustion, his thought flames up into praise,

> How rich are the depths of God—how deep his wisdom and knowledge—and how impossible to penetrate his motives or understand his methods! Who could ever know the mind of the Lord? Who could ever

be his counsellor? Who could ever give him anything or lend him anything? All that exists comes from him; all is by him and for him. To him be glory forever! Amen (Romans 11:33–6).

The depths of God—the phrase makes Paul curiously contemporary. Current religious writing tends to warn us against a God up there or a God out there; tends to guide our minds instead to concepts like the ground of our being, our ultimate and deepest concern. It is of course only a change of metaphor, for depths is just as much a metaphor, however useful, as up there or out there. But it is a common enough Pauline metaphor; one need only go to I Corinthians to see how much it means to Paul, 'The Spirit reaches the depths of everything, even the depths of God . . . the depths of God can be known only by the Spirit of God' (I Corinthians 2:10–11). I expect it was Paul's example at least as much as his own genius that made this a favourite metaphor for John of the Cross. In *The Living Flame* for example, 'Thou that tenderly woundest my soul in its deepest centre'.

For John it is in the deepest centre of the soul that God must be sought and found. In the *Spiritual Canticle* there is Stanza 36 and John's commentary upon it,

And then we shall go forth.
To the lofty caverns of the rock . . .

The lofty caverns are the lofty and high and deep mysteries in the wisdom of God which are in Christ . . . For he is like an abundant mine with many recesses containing treasures which, for all that men try to fathom them, the end and bottom is never reached.

Another example of Paul slipping into prayer, interesting for a different reason, is to be found in II Corinthians. Paul is appealing quite frankly for money. He wants, to put it bluntly, to put up the collection. It is a helpful chapter for any Christian minister who has to get into a pulpit and do a job—asking for money—highly distasteful to most of us. It helps to be reminded that Paul had to do it, too. But just at the end of his money talk, the fact that he is asking for a gift suddenly reminds Paul of God's greatest gift—his

53

Son Jesus Christ. And he breaks immediately and spontaneously into prayer, 'Thanks be to God for his inexpressible gift' (II Corinthians 9:15). Rather like the head of King Charles in one of the Dickens novels, no matter what Paul is thinking or writing about, prayer will keep breaking in.

But the supreme example of how Paul slips from prose into prayer and back again is his Letter to the Ephesians which, I imagine, most would accept as also representing the highest reach of Pauline thought. I can never make up my mind whether this Letter is best described as prose frequently rising into prayer or prayer occasionally dropping into prose. Here quotation is useless; the only thing to do is to read it and realise afresh how prayer and thought intermingle. Paul can hardly finish the initial greeting before he breaks into his great prayer of praise. I sometimes wonder why the Church and we, its members, don't use this great opening prayer more. For me at any rate, in the New Testament it comes only after the Our Father and Christ's prayer at the Last Supper; also perhaps the *Magnificat*. I think this opening prayer in Ephesians is especially and splendidly suitable for thanksgiving after Holy Communion. At the beginning of Chapter 3 Paul seems about to break into prayer again but something strikes him that he wants to say. He says it and then, halfway down the chapter, he resumes his prayer. But in regard to Ephesians, there is no point in quotation. One can only say in the words of Augustine, *'Tolle lege'*.

Ephesians is, as far as our human vision can reach, the high peak of Pauline prayer. But there is another peak, far beyond our seeing and we learn of it only from ten or eleven lines in II Corinthians,

Must I go on boasting, though there is nothing to be gained by it? But I will move on to the visions and revelations I have had from the Lord. I know a man in Christ who, fourteen years ago, was caught up—whether still in the body or out of the body I do not know; God knows—right into the third heaven. I do know, however, that this same person—whether in the body or out of the body I do not know; God knows—was caught up into paradise and heard things which must not and cannot be put into human language (II Corinthians 12:1–4).

Cannot be put into human language! That is always the message from the invisible peaks. In his Prologue to *The Living Flame*, John of the Cross, puts it, 'Of my own power I can say naught that is of any value, specially in things of such sublimity.' At the end of *The Living Flame* he gives up even the effort, 'I see clearly I cannot say aught concerning it . . . and for that reason I leave speaking of it here.'

Paul and John were both masters of words. They differ in a thousand ways, the great Apostle and the great contemplative. But when it comes to the ultimate wordlessness, Paul and John are at one. There are no further words. There is only the Word.

*

Some of the Pauline texts I have just been quoting could give the impression that Paul prayed only for his Christians. This derives from the nature of his Letters, most of them hurried missives to his Christian communities and naturally dealing chiefly with the things intimately concerning both them and him. But even from these intimate Letters, Paul's perspective on prayer emerges as much wider than that. He spent a lot of his life quarrelling with his kinsmen, the Jews, but 'I have the very warmest love for the Jews, and I pray to God for them to be saved' (Romans 10:1). We get another glimpse of a wider prayer when Paul addresses a mixed audience of Jews and Romans at Caesarea, in the presence of King Agrippa and his wife Bernice. Agrippa, impressed, says to Paul, 'A little more and your arguments would make a Christian of me.' Paul replies: 'I wish before God that not only you but all who have heard me today would come to be as I am, except for these chains' (Acts 26:28–9). It is reminder that whatever mixed or motley audience Paul spoke to all the way from Jerusalem to Illyricum, he ·prayed for them just as earnestly as he preached. He seems almost to identify these two strands of his apostolate in Romans, 'The God I worship spiritually by preaching the Good News of his Son knows that I never fail to mention you in my prayers' (Romans 1:9). Prayer giving fuel to preaching, preaching irrigated by prayer—that was the Pauline formula, hardly less valid today.

But to get the real universalism of early Christian prayer, one must go to I Timothy and the words the author puts on the lips of Paul.

> My advice is that, first of all, there should be prayers offered for everyone—petitions, intercessions and thanksgivings—and especially for kings and others in authority, so that we may be able to live religious and reverent lives in peace and quiet. To do this is right, and will please God our saviour; he wants everyone to be saved and to reach full knowledge of the truth (I Timothy 2:1–4).

Right from the beginning the Prayer of the Church was prayer for the world.

PART THREE

Paul and Christ

Chapter VI

'WHO ARE YOU, LORD?' (ACTS 9:4)

Writing to Philippi, Paul coined one of his most famous phrases, 'Life to me, of course, is Christ' (Philippians 1:21). Paul could have said with even greater truth, 'Prayer to me, of course, is Christ.' From the topic of Paul's prayer it is natural, indeed inescapable, to go on to speak of Paul's relationship with Christ.

Three times in Acts we read Paul's Damascus question, 'Who are you, Lord?'

'Who are you, Lord?' The question is a question of forever. It has been and remains on the lips of many before and after Paul. The emissaries of John the Baptist ask, 'Are you the one who is to come or have we got to wait for someone else?' (Matthew 11:3.) We hear the question from the enemies of Christ, 'How much longer are you going to keep us in suspense? If you are the Christ, tell us plainly' (John 10:24). A fearful Pilate was only re-phrasing the question when he re-entered the Praetorium and said to Jesus, 'Where do you come from?' (John 19:9.) Most solemnly of all it was put by the High Priest presiding over the trial of Christ, 'I put you on oath by the living God to tell us if you are the Christ, the Son of God' (Matthew 26:63). The murmur of the question has pervaded the Christian centuries. In our own age of rock music the instinct of the authors of *Jesus Christ Superstar* led them to clothe this same never-quite-forgotten question in the (for me at any rate) one haunting melody of the rock opera,

Jesus Christ, Jesus Christ
Who are you, what have you sacrificed?
Jesus Christ Superstar
Do you think you're what they say you are?

59

I expect there are many kinds of inspiration, none of them untouched by the Holy Spirit.

'Who are you Lord?' There was of course an immediate answer, partially understood. But I think there is a sense in which Paul spent the rest of his life fathoming the answer to his own question. From this point on there was only one sun in Paul's sky, Christ. But the sun was too bright, too great and initially too bewildering to be immediately comprehended. It is impossible to read Paul's Letters without seeing his life as a continued, dazzled gazing at this splendid sun. He says as much in II Corinthians where, comparing the first *'Let there be light'* of Genesis to the coming of the Saviour, he goes on immediately to talk about 'the glory on the face of Christ' (II Corinthians 4:6). A phrase like this is not just Paul reflecting. It is Paul remembering and trying to describe the avalanche of glory that came into his life at Damascus.

It is useful to reflect on Paul's first experience of the Risen Christ. It surely must have been a feeling of total helplessness in the presence of overwhelming power. The dazzling light, brighter (Luke tells us) than the noonday sun, came inexorably down from heaven and enveloped himself and his companions. The light was so dazzling that Paul was suddenly blind. With the light there was an irresistible power that flung Paul and his companions to the ground. And then there was the voice around them like a bursting sea, the voice Paul would never forget, 'Saul, Saul, why are you persecuting me?' (Acts 9:4.)

Blinded by the light, deafened by the voice, flung down by the mysterious power, Paul's immediate instinctive reaction must have been one of fear bordering on terror. There is a good deal of evidence in Scripture and Christian tradition that this is a common initial reaction to a sudden eruption of the divine. The sight of the angel in the temple 'disturbed Zechariah and he was overcome with fear' (Luke 1:12). Mary, when the angel spoke to her at the Annunciation, is described as 'deeply disturbed' (Luke 1:29). When the angel of the Lord appeared to Luke's hillside shepherds 'the glory of the Lord shone about them. They were terrified' (Luke 2:9). After the Resurrection the women at the empty tomb, confronted with 'two men in brilliant clothes were 'terrified . . . lowered their eyes' (Luke 24:4–5). On the Resurrection evening, when the Risen Christ stood for the first time among his own, 'In a state of alarm and fright they thought they were seeing a ghost' (Luke 24:36). Christian history offers the same witness. Teresa of Avila, for example, writes in Chapter 28 of her Life,

O my Jesus if one could but describe the majesty with which Thou doth reveal Thyself. How completely art Thou Lord of the whole world and of the Heavens and of a thousand other worlds and of countless worlds and Heavens that Thou has created And the majesty with which thou dost reveal Thyself shows the soul that to be Lord of this is nothing for Thee.

Christian poetry can catch the same truth and Gerard Manley Hopkins in *The Wreck of the Deutschland* has lines that apply readily to Paul and Damascus,

Wring thy rebel, dogged in den,
Man's malice, with wrecking and storm.
Beyond saying sweet, past telling of tongue,
Thou art lightning and love, I found it, a
    winter and warm;
Father and fondler of hearts thou has wrung;
Hast thy dark descending and most art merciful then.

Wring thy rebel! The phrase sums up Paul well as the great rebel lies there, blind, confused, helpless, his world suddenly turned upside down and inside out by his first experience of Christ the Son of the living God. Later on he would come to understand that there really was no need to be afraid; the overmastering power, however terrifying, was only the encircling arms of the love of God. But it would appear that before God can safely unveil himself to a creature as infinite love, there is a need for the creature to experience him as irresistible power. I expect this is just another way of saying that humility is the foundation of all the virtues. That, no doubt, was the foundation Christ wished to lay when he let Paul experience what it is to fall into the hands of the living God. Paul, many years later, would write lyrically about the love of God made visible in Christ Jesus, our Lord. At Damascus it was rather the power of God made tangible in Christ Jesus, our Lord.

61

It is abundantly clear from Paul's Letters that this experience of the power of God in Christ remained indelibly stamped on his mind. That first Damascus thrill of power and helplessness surfaces again and again. We find an early example in II Thessalonians when Paul is speaking of the Second Coming of Christ, 'He will come in flaming fire . . . It will be their punishment to be lost eternally, excluded from the presence of the Lord and the glory of His strength' (II Thessalonians 1:8–9).

At the summit of his thought in Ephesians his sense (or should one say his memory?) of the power of God is still fresh: he reminds the Ephesians 'how infinitely great is the power that he has exercised for us believers. This you can tell from the strength of his power at work in Christ' (Ephesians 1:19–20). But nowhere does Paul's sense of his own weakness, and its irrelevance when considered in the context of Christ's power, emerge so memorably as in II Corinthians,

> About this thing, I have pleaded with the Lord three times for it to leave me but he has said 'My grace is enough for you; my power is at its best in weakness. So I shall be very happy to make my weaknesses my special boast so that the power of Christ may stay over me (II Corinthians 12:8–9).

That is the story of Paul's life: helplessness that did not matter at all because of the presence and power of Christ. The first big lesson in the long, hard school of humility had come to Paul as he lay there prostrate and almost stunned, listening to a voice that rebuked, *'Saul, Saul, why are you persecuting me?'*

I have delayed a good deal, perhaps too long, on this aspect of Damascus; Paul indescribably, unforgettably, confronted with the power and majesty of the Risen Lord. But the more I read Acts and the Letters the more I am convinced that the Damascus experience provides one valuable key to an understanding of Paul. Both in his outlook and his life we meet an audacity so remarkable that one seeks for some bolder word to describe the reality. For instance there is the calm fashion, his enemies would have said the insolent fashion, in which he takes it for granted that this message of his is destined to spread, indeed is already spreading, all over the world.

All over the Pauline Letters we find this audacity of universalism. For him there are no boundaries to the Gospel except those of the human race.

And why is Paul so consistently audacious? The key to his audacity is found in words Paul wrote to Colossae: 'You will have in you the strength, based on his own glorious power, never to give in' (Colossians 1:11). His own glorious power! Paul is still remembering Damascus, and if God be with us, who is against us?

*

This experience, however, was only a starting point. It initiated a relationship with Christ which, while never ceasing to be a relationship of dependence, increasingly became a relationship of deeper knowledge and more passionate love. The more Paul gazed at the glory that was Christ the more he understood; yet the more he understood, the more he was dazzled. But his vision, far from being a purely contemplative vision untouched by reality, was constantly enriched and corrected by his daily experience of apostolate, especially perhaps by the trials and tensions of apostolate. He had to look at 'God in Christ reconciling the world to himself' (II Corinthians 5:19) in order to understand the destiny of man. But equally he had to focus on the reality of man (as he does, for example, in Chapters 1 and 2 of Romans) in order to understand the purposes of God and exalt his unending mercy. He was supremely the contemplative of brass tacks, of gritty and sometimes grimy reality. But the direction of his journey remained constant: towards the summit he speaks of to the Ephesians, 'until, knowing the love of Christ, which is beyond all knowledge, you are filled with the utter fullness of God' (Ephesians 3:19).

Paul's Letters, like Paul's life, are totally Christ-centred. Christ is stamped on almost every page. The banal level of arithmetic is perhaps useful in order to bring home the deeper reality. I have open before me as I write that section of the New Testament containing the Pauline Letters. It comprises 94 pages. There are only four of these pages without the name of Christ. In Romans,

63

the name of Christ or some obvious synonym occurs on an average five times on each page. For Colossians the average is seven; for I Corinthians, six; for II Corinthians, six; for Galatians, seven; for Ephesians, nine; for I Thessalonians, seven; for II Thessalonians, eight. Still on this level of arithmetic, the Letter to the Philippians has, with Ephesians, the highest average; the name of Christ occurs nine times on each page. On one page of Philippians the name occurs thirteen times. All natural enough when you come to think of it. Love letters tend to be concerned with somebody you love.

But if every Letter tells us about Paul's love for Christ, each of them has its own emphasis inside Paul's growing understanding of Christ and the Christian mystery. The emphasis is influenced by several factors: the reason behind a particular Letter; the circumstances of the people to whom it was written: and, perhaps most important of all, what aspect of Christ was uppermost in Paul's mind at the time. Concerning each Letter I look at here, I ask the same question. What, whether he himself was conscious of it or not at the time, was at the top of Paul's mind when he wrote this particular Letter? What is the underlying concern or insight which, because it keeps surfacing through the Letter, was probably just then dominating Paul's mind?

I and II Thessalonians

Before going on to the central concern of these two Letters, Paul's earliest, a word about the Letters themselves. The two of them, the first somewhat more than the second, are first-love Letters. Although there are lots of troubles around, everything in Paul's garden is lovely and he can hardly find words warm enough to praise his Thessalonian converts,

> You were led to become imitators of us, and of the Lord; and it was with the joy of the Holy Spirit that you took to the gospel, in spite of the great opposition all around you. This has made you the great example to all believers in Macedonia and Achaia (I Thessalonians 1:6–7).

This is the tune which Paul lyrically sings again and again throughout these two Letters. They remind me of the familiar verse

When all the world is young, lad
And all the grass is green
And every goose a swan, lad
And every lass a queen.

For Paul just then the grass was very green in Thessalonika. It would wither a lot before, writing to the Philippians in AD 56, he would reflect sadly, 'All the rest seem more interested in themselves than in Jesus Christ' (Philippians 2:21). By AD 56 there are a lot of geese around! It is hardly likely that there were only swans in Thessalonika and only geese in Ephesus. It seems more likely that for Paul, as for many another after him, early and naïve illusions had been tempered by a decade of apostolate. But it is touching to find Paul writing to the Thessalonians in much the same vein as a young missionary, full of enthusiasm, writing his first letters home from Korea or Chile or Nigeria or wherever it may be. The letters may tell you little enough about the full reality of Korea or Chile or Nigeria. They tell you a lot about the marvel of being young and full of ideals, courage and hope. It is hard to better springtime and among the Pauline Letters, Thessalonika is spring.

These two Letters to the Thessalonians remind me of spring in another and quite different way. In spring you get the first hint of what the harvest will be in September, the young shoots that will later be grain or fruit or whatever. And here in these two Letters you get the young shoots of doctrine which will later blossom into the full harvest of Romans or Ephesians. In fact, if Paul in the years AD 48–9 had decided to make some rough notes to be the basis of his later teaching, I doubt if he could have done much better than these two short Letters to Thessalonika. In germ and bud, all or nearly all is there. As soon as his salutation in I Thessalonians is over, Paul at once begins, 'We know, brothers, that God loves you' (1:4)—it is the first striking of a chord that will ultimately dominate the whole Pauline symphony. Everything flows from that. The Holy Spirit, another key doctrine in Paul, is mentioned twice in the first twelve lines. Another central Pauline concept is that of death—resurrection in and with Christ. We find it succinctly put in I Thessalonians, 'We believe that Jesus Christ died and rose again, and that it will be the same for those who have died in Jesus; God will bring them with him' (4:14). Later on Paul will expand on that, will dress it up in this or that metaphor but the basic idea will remain the same. This is true of most of the leading Pauline ideas. They are found in embryonic form in Thessalonians I and II, and we meet them developed, luxuriant, sometimes flamboyant, but still essentially the same in the fully grown Pauline tree. Paul's vision grew but deep down it didn't really change.

One thing that did change was the relative importance of one concept as related to another. This could change a great deal as Paul sorted his ideas out over the years. These two Letters offer an excellent example. There is little doubt what aspect of Christ was chiefly in Paul's mind when he wrote to the Thessalonians; certainly they and almost certainly he were primarily thinking of the Christ who had said he would come again in glory to judge the wicked, to bring his friends home. As far as the Thessalonians were concerned, the sooner the better, and the Letters are full of an expectation that it might be quite soon. These two Letters always remind me—I hope I am not being irreverent—of the atmosphere of a group of people in an arrival lounge at an airport, waiting for a VIP to come in. A problem, almost a protocol problem, occurs to somebody: what about the Christians who have died? Isn't it rather a shame they can't be part of this welcoming committee? Paul reassures them. The dead they are worrying about will be actually the first to meet the arriving Christ; they are already, so to speak, out there on the tarmac. But the arriving Lord is the dominating concept. The foreseeable future is, in Paul's own words, 'So we shall stay with the Lord forever' (I Thessalonians 4:17), a bit like Peter on Thabor and his 'Lord it is wonderful for us to be here' (Mark 9:5). The Second Letter to the Thessalonians is still concerned with the arriving Christ but here Paul is flashing a warning on the TV screen. The plane is delayed, perhaps indefinitely, further bulletins later. In the meantime, what is everybody to do? Just wait around? That this inclination was present is clear from II Thessalonians, 'Now we hear there are some of you living in idleness, doing no work themselves but interfering with everyone else's' (3:11)—clearly some of the swans are losing a little of their plumage!

The Lord of power, the Lord of the Second Coming—that was the aspect of Christ most in Paul's mind when he wrote I and II Thessalonians. It never disappears from his mind; we find it cropping up again and again throughout his Letters. I believe one can detect a growth in Paul's vision of the Second Coming. At a later stage his mind dwells more easily on a Christ who is everything and in everything. In Colossians he speaks of 'Christ among you your hope of glory', more a Lord who is mysteriously present and will duly reveal himself than a Christ who has gone away and should shortly be on the passenger list back. He is already, so to speak, in the airport. Indeed properly understood he actually is the airport. But just like the veils that fell from Paul's eyes in Damascus, veils still darker must fall before he or any other can fully see the Lord who is Spirit. In later Paul I think the emphasis changes on another point: it is no longer so much a question of Christ's coming to us, rather a question of our going to Christ. Which is as it should be. The iron filings fly to the magnet, not the other way around.

Philippians

The Letter to the Philippians was written possibly in AD 56. It is a window into Paul's mind and heart some twenty years after Damascus. Paul, in jail somewhere (the scholars don't seem certain just where), isn't quite sure whether his imprisonment will end in release or in death. This puts this unique Pauline Letter in the same *genre* of jail literature as, for instance, *The Prisoner of Chillon, The Ballad of Reading Jail* or (for an Irishman) nearer home, Brendan Behan's *The Quare Fella*. But if I were to choose a line from English literature to sum up Philippians I would not go to any of these obvious analogues but to a favourite line from *Murder in the Cathedral*, where Thomas à Becket says, 'And I am not in danger, only near to death.'

That conveys the whole atmosphere of Philippians. Any step coming down the corridor may well be the step of an official setting Paul free—or the step of the executioner. Paul may never again see or write to his children at Philippi who more than any others (cf.

Philippians 4:15) had been generous to him in times of need.

Philippians, then, is a unique unveiling of Paul's heart. By comparison with some of the other Letters it tells us little about Paul's mind. From it we learn how much Christ meant to Paul. We don't learn very much about Paul's understanding of Christ or his growth in that understanding apart from the christological hymn of Chapter 2 which Paul, it would appear, borrowed from the liturgy of the time. If one thinks of Christ as the starry sky at night, Philippians is mostly poetry, only in a passing way astronomy. For the astronomy we must go to other Letters. Not that in Paul we ever get pure poetry or pure astronomy. The lover keeps breaking in on the theologian all the time and so does the theologian on the lover. The mixture varies from one Letter to another.

So this Letter of farewell is a time for opening his heart to his friends, rather like what the Last Supper was for Christ. Paul will keep nothing back. He tells them how much they mean to him, 'God knows how much I miss you all, loving you as Christ Jesus loves you' (1:8). He reminds them what he most wants from them, 'If our life in Christ means anything to you, if love can persuade at all, or the Spirit that we have in common, or any tenderness and sympathy, then be united in your convictions and united in your love' (2:2). It is a Pauline echo of Christ's command, 'Love one another as I have loved you' (John 15:12). He underlines for them what, in spite of the inevitable trials and persecutions, must be the unchanging atmosphere of their Christian lives: 'I want you to be happy, always happy in the Lord; I repeat, what I want is your happiness' (Philippians 4:4). Again it sounds very like an echo of the words John attributes to Christ at the Last Supper, 'you are sad now but I shall see you again, and your hearts will be full of joy, and that joy no one shall take from you' (John 16:22).

Indeed it is uncanny how the resonances of the Last Supper constantly emerge in Philippians. I sometimes wonder if, in some sense, Paul may have read Chapters 13 to 17 of St John's Gospel. I understand that some scholars, since the Qumran documents, now tend to place the first version of John's Gospel almost as early as that of Mark. That could bring some form of these incomparable Johannine chapters within the life of Paul. Anyhow it would appear almost a miracle if Paul, the world traveller, never met and talked to John. It is easy to imagine what or rather whom they would talk about. They could hardly avoid the Last Supper, and I keep feeling whenever I read Philippians that Paul had that most lovely of farewells in mind when he dictated his own farewell to the Christian community at Philippi.

A moment, then, for keeping nothing back. Least of all would he wish to keep back how Christ had come completely to dominate his life. Philippians, therefore, is a rich glimpse into Paul's heart some twenty years after the bewildered question of Damascus, and Paul's heart lies completely unveiled in the third chapter. If all but, say, six short passages of Paul were to be irretrievably lost in some nuclear cataclysm, I think most Paul-lovers would choose this passage as among the six to be preserved.

> Nothing can happen that will outweigh the supreme advantage of knowing Christ Jesus my Lord. For him I have accepted the loss of everything, and I look on everything as so much rubbish if only I can have Christ and be given a place in him. I am no longer trying for perfection by my own efforts, the perfection that comes from the Law, but I want only the perfection that comes through faith in Christ, and is from God and based on faith. All I want is to know Christ and the power of his resurrection and to share his sufferings by reproducing the pattern of his death' (3:8–10).

A passage like this needs no comment, indeed bears no comment. One can only read it, ponder it again and again and try, with perhaps a hint of envy, to grasp something of what Christ had come to mean to Paul. In other Pauline Letters we get more about the theology of Christ, his place in the process of justification, how he is the centre of the cosmos, the focus of salvation history, the alpha and omega, the beginning and the end. But nowhere do we get so inescapably as here in Philippians the shining picture of how totally Christ had come to possess Paul's life. By comparison everything else was rubbish. The Latin has a stronger word, *stercora*, which can fairly be translated as dung. Paul was utterly and completely in love with Christ. Not that he had forgotten the onrush of power in Damascus; here in Philippians we find this memory of Christ's power associated with the probability of death around the corner.

69

For us, our homeland is in heaven, and from heaven comes the saviour we are waiting for, the Lord Jesus Christ, and he will transform these wretched bodies of ours into copies of his glorious body. He will do that by the same power with which he will subdue the whole universe (3:20).

But if the memory of power is still vivid, it is now seen as at the service of a transforming love *'that will transform these wretched bodies of ours into copies of his glorious body'*. In spite of hesitations, I had almost said polite hesitations, a few verses back, Paul is so enviably sure!

This same total loving preoccupation with Christ is already found just as movingly in the first chapter of Philippians. His thought seems to play for a moment with the dread possibility that under torture or threat of death he might deny Christ. But he immediately turns from this unthinkable abyss.

My one hope and trust is that I shall never have to admit defeat but that now as always I shall have the courage for Christ to be glorified in my body, whether by my life or by my death. Life to me, of course, is Christ . . . I want to be gone and be with Christ which would be very much the better, but for me to stay alive in the body is a more urgent need for your sake (1:20f).

'Life to me, of course, is Christ'—if we search for a seven-word summary of Pauline and Christian spirituality we could do worse than that. Indeed it is impossible to do better. Twenty years of living in Christ's presence, pondering his mysteries and preaching his Gospel had brought Paul's mind, often over the path of great suffering, into a constant vivid awareness of what one can only call the omnipresence of Christ and his redeeming and transforming love. Whatever vista Paul looked up at, in heaven or on earth, there was only 'the glory on the face of Christ' (II Corinthians 4:6).

'Life to me, of course, is Christ'—this self-summary of Paul's spirituality is relevant to any renewal of Christian spirituality today. Of the various criticisms levelled against spirituality as encouraged in seminaries and novitiates until a few decades ago, one frequently recurring is that it tended to create people for whom the spiritual life consisted largely in careful bit-in-the-teeth fidelity to a programme of spiritual exercises. Provided you regularly ticked off your

meditation, your spiritual reading, your visit, your rosary, your assorted examinations of conscience and the rest, God remained pleased in his heaven and all was right with your spiritual world. Thus presented, this picture of an earlier spirituality is of course a caricature. At any rate it is a caricature of the spirituality I personally encountered in a seminary of the late thirties. This spirituality, while undoubtedly stressing, perhaps over-stressing, the importance of a programme of spiritual exercises, nevertheless set this programme in a much wider and saner Christian context. Still, any worthwhile caricature derives its quality from exaggerating something really there. De Gaulle's nose did exist. In that sense there is some validity in the criticism. In the spirituality many of us grew up in there was too much emphasis on fidelity to a programme.

For Paul Christian spirituality was never preoccupation with a programme. It meant rather to be dominated, captivated by a person. It means just the same thing today. The central irreplaceable thing is to try to grow towards a state where we will, with some sincerity, be able to say with Paul, *'Life to me, of course, is Christ.'* By comparison with this, all methods, all approaches in spirituality are relatively unimportant. If these help towards this central thing they are to be welcomed. If they hinder this central thing, above all if they ever seek to usurp the place of this central thing, then they are useless and dangerous. We have very little evidence in Paul of any kind of spiritual programme. We have evidence on almost every page of his Letters that for him Christ was everything and in everything.

Does this mean that the old programme approach was misguided and should be discarded? I think that at this point the debate is sometimes trivialised when it is seriously suggested that here alone, against all common human experience, something important can be achieved without some sort of programme or system. If a man wants, for instance, to play great music, he will not achieve it without endless demanding practice, in other words without a programme. The same is true of painting a good picture or writing a worthwhile book. Much the same is true in the area of human relationships. The friends we drift away from are those we vaguely invite to visit us sometime. It's different if we say, 'What about dropping in next Tuesday evening at 7 o'clock for a bite and a chat;

71

or if Tuesday doesn't suit, Wednesday.' If Jack and Jill are getting serious about each other they will not be content to say vaguely on parting, 'Well, we'll see each other around.' There will be a place to meet and in every sense a date. The vague, unstructured and imprecise, often an excuse for laziness or lack of real interest, can be a very insidious enemy of accomplishment or growth. I believe it is right to have the greatest scepticism about a vague, imprecise and unstructured approach to the supremely important matter of knowing and loving Jesus Christ our Lord. As Bonhoeffer puts it,

> Some meditation on the Scripture, prayer and intercession are a service we owe; and because the grace of God is found in this service, we should train ourselves to set apart a regular hour for it. For the pastor it is an indispensable duty and his whole ministry will depend upon it (*Life Together*, SCM, p.66).

In other words, we are back to a programme, a programme, of course, totally subordinated to a person, but nevertheless a programme. No doubt the programme was often too rigid, too static, not allowing enough for human differences or even for a Holy Spirit, of endlessly rich variety. Sometimes meticulous fidelity to a programme could produce smugness about a duty fulfilled rather than real growth in holiness although this may often have been due more to temperament rather than a lack in the programme. Where can we usefully look for guidelines that will keep us and our programme sane?

I suggest that the answer to that question is also to be found in Philippians. Just after Paul tells them, 'In your minds you must be the same as Christ Jesus' (2:5) he breaks at once into his christological hymn. I like to think of this hymn as Paul's Meditation Book. The outlines are not very different from the Spiritual Exercises of St Ignatius: both are a sustained and loving gaze at the mysteries of Christ Incarnate, Crucified and Risen. If this is at the heart of whatever programme we map out, the details will take care of themselves.

Here is Paul's Meditation Book,

His state was divine

yet he did not cling
to his equality with God
but emptied himself
to assume the condition of a slave,
and became as men are;
and being as all men are,
he was humbler yet,
even to accepting death,
death on a cross.
But God raised him high
and gave him the name
which is above all other names
so that all beings
in the heavens, on earth and in the underworld,
should bend the knee at the name of Jesus
and that every tongue should acclaim
Jesus Christ as Lord
to the glory of God the Father (Philippians 2:6–11).

'Life to me, of course, is Christ.'

How are we to grow towards this? Near the heart of the answer is a truth of Vatican II, 'the Eucharist is the source and centre of priestly life' (PO 14). This truth, if directed especially to those of us who are priests, has, I suggest, a real relevance for all Christians. It *almost* entitles us to say, 'Life to me, of course, is the Eucharist.' Almost, but not quite, for Christ comes to us in other garments too. Still this phrase, modelled on that of Paul, encapsulates an important truth about Christian spirituality. It is easy to recall Abbot Marmion in his later years, 'I live now by my daily Holy Communion.' The Eucharist incomparably plunges us into the Paschal Mysteries that fill Paul's christological hymn in Philippians.

Chapter VII

THE CHRIST OF CORINTHIANS

I Corinthians

When Paul began writing his First Letter to the Corinthians, his mind seems to have been haunted by the thought of the Crucified Christ. After a reference to the division among the Corinthians, ' "I am for Paul," "I am for Apollos," "I am for Cephas," "I am for Christ" ' (I Corinthians 1:12), he turns on them almost savagely and demands, 'Was it Paul that was crucified for you?' (1:13). A few verses later he defines his mission,

> to preach the Good News and not to preach that in terms of philosophy in which the crucifixion of Christ cannot be expressed. The language of the cross may be illogical to those who are not on the way to salvation, but those of us who are on the way see it as God's power to save (1:17).

While Jews demand miracles and Greeks look for wisdom 'here are we preaching a crucified Christ . . . a Christ who is the power and wisdom of God' (1:22). In the second chapter, still talking about the message he had brought, he tells them, indeed boasts to them, 'The only knowledge I claimed to have was about Jesus, and only about him as the crucified Christ' (2:2). A few verses further on he is speaking of the unwisdom of 'the masters of this age . . . or they would not have crucified the Lord of Glory' (2:8).

These two early chapters of I Corinthians are Paul's longest and most sustained meditation on the Passion and Death of our Lord. Not that passion is absent elsewhere; indeed throughout the Pauline letters it is never far away from his thoughts. It is the background

74

to everything: God so loved the world. Paul, even though the Christ he had met was the Risen Christ, was always Paul of the Cross. Peter and John could lovingly remember. Paul, like the rest of us, could lovingly meditate. He would have readily agreed with Teresa of Avila when she described Christ's Passion as always and everywhere the source of everything that is good.

It is interesting and suggestive about the ultimate texture of Paul's mind that this First Letter to the Corinthians, which begins with Paul's most sustained meditation on the Crucifixion, should find its climax in Chapter 15, in Paul's most sustained meditation on the Resurrection. Perhaps it was a conscious decision of Paul to balance his emphasis on the suffering Christ at the beginning by emphasising the Risen and glorious Christ at the end. But I do not think so. Paul wasn't that kind of balancing writer; it just poured out as he felt it. And if we get this clear balance in I Corinthians, I think it is because this was simply the shape in Paul's mind; death and resurrection, in Christ and in us, being for him the shape of reality. In between the Passion Meditation at the beginning of this Letter and the Resurrection Meditation at the end, Paul squeezes in a whole panorama of Christian questions, Christian answers, Christian teaching, Christian ideals. There is profound teaching on the Spirit; a ruling about a case of incest; guidance about litigation among Christians; matters of marriage and virginity; some instructions about food sacrificed to idols; the earliest written reference to the Eucharist; a description of the Christian community as the Spirit-filled and therefore charity-marked community. A miniature of Christian life, but fixed firmly between the two poles of Christ's Death and his Resurrection. Whether Paul planned it that way or not, the shape of the Letter is a profound reminder how Christ's Paschal Mysteries surround and penetrate all Christian living.

Still, it is a different aspect of Christ that Paul was primarily concerned with when he wrote these pages, so vibrant and so full of real, spiky, intractable life. This aspect is our unity with Christ and, as a consequence, our need for unity with one another. That this unity was seriously threatened emerges in the opening lines, 'All the same I do appeal to you, brothers, to make up the differences between you, and instead of disagreeing among yourselves, to be united again in belief and practice' (1:10). This was Paul's chief preoccupation when he wrote the Letter. The same underlying concern surfaces again when he talks about their meetings to celebrate the Eucharist, 'In the first place, I hear that when you all come together as a community, there are separate factions among you, and I half believe it' (11:18). Unity broken or seriously threatened, how to restore and safeguard it—that was the problem facing Paul. His letter is full of his answer. Christ and they are one; how can they shatter or threaten this unity given by God? I quote some examples.

The first is in a sort of postscript to his introductory greeting, 'God by calling you has JOINED you to his Son, Jesus Christ; and God is faithful' (1:9). The unspoken question is: God is faithful but what about you? At the end of the first chapter Paul tells them, 'But you, God has made members of Christ Jesus and by God's doing he has become our wisdom, and our virtue, and our holiness, and our freedom. As scripture says, 'if anyone wants to boast, let him boast about the Lord' (1:31). So, clearly the message runs, drop this silly and divisive boasting about belonging to Apollos, Cephas or Paul; whatever you have, you have in corporate fashion as members of Christ Jesus. In Chapter 3 he uses the metaphor of a building to re-emphasise their structural inbuilt unity with Christ and therefore with one another. 'For the foundation nobody can lay other than the one which has already been laid, that is Jesus Christ' (3:11). In Chapter 6, he is talking about fornication, a topic rather removed from unity with Christ, but a detail like that doesn't stop Paul hammering home his central thesis, 'You know, surely, that your bodies are members making up the body of Christ; do you think I can take parts of Christ's body and join them to the body of a prostitute? . . . anyone who is joined to the Lord is one spirit with him' (6:15). In Chapter 8 he is talking about something quite different, the scandal one may give to an uninformed brother by eating meat sacrificed to idols. Again the idea of the Christian's quasi-identity with Christ breaks compulsively in, 'In this way your knowledge could become the ruin of someone weak, of a brother for whom Christ died. By sinning in this way against your brothers . . . it would be Christ against whom you have sinned' (8:11–12). All these almost random references to the unity between Christ and his members are, if you like, rather like the orchestra before the curtain goes up, giving you bits and snatches of the opera ahead. For in Chapter 12, Paul formally takes up the topic of the Christian's identity with Christ in a passage which is the first serious attempt to put in words the concept of the Mystical Body. Perhaps we are too familiar with the passage to realise how startling one word is as Paul introduces the topic, 'Just as a human body, though it is made up of many parts, is a single unit because all these parts, though many, make one body, so it is with Christ' (12:12). With *Christ*! We might have expected Paul to say so it is with *the Church*, the Church is rather like that. But he doesn't say the Church; he says so it is with *Christ*. For Paul, after Damascus, Christ was always the *whole* Christ, head and members united in a mysterious unity which Paul, for all his genius, has been able only to convey rather than to explain fully, 'Now you together are Christ's body; but each of you is a different part of it' (12:27). And Paul goes on to Chapter 13, ever quoted, ever beautiful, telling us for all time of the charity binding the members of Christ's Body together. Chapter 15, where Paul talks about the Resurrection is, of course, a continuation of the same theme. For Paul is talking about the Resurrection of the *whole* Christ. Indeed he gets angry at the idea that Christ could rise alone, 'how can some of you be saying that there is no resurrection of the dead? If there is no resurrection of the dead, Christ himself cannot have been raised' (15:12). We are back to 1:9 where Paul laid down what I might call the thesis or motif of I Corinthians, *'God by calling you has joined you to his Son, Jesus Christ.'* The motif sounded in the first chapter recurs repeatedly throughout the Letter, finds its *fortissimo* in Chapter 12 and is triumphantly thundered out again in Chapter 15. What God has joined together, let no man put asunder.

The First Letter to the Corinthians is very much a Letter for Christians today. Corinth, in so many ways, was a microcosm of much that we have been experiencing in recent decades. The Christian community of Corinth was riddled with factions and divisions. Inside my own Church today, factions and divisions are unmistakable. In the wider area of Christendom, we have all become more conscious of the scandal of disunity. We face today, on a world scale, much the same problems as Paul faced in Corinth. His answers for Corinth are worth pondering on for ourselves. The core of his answer was to point to a God-given, grace-filled reality, 'God by calling you has joined you to his Son, Jesus Christ' (1:9). However indispensable human effort and striving for unity are, the real hope of unity always remains what it was for Paul, 'You, God has made members of Christ Jesus and by God's doing he has become our wisdom and our virtue, and our holiness, and our freedom' (1:30).

Still, the human effort must go on, often taking the form of debate inside the Catholic Church, discussion with Christians and others outside it. A final lesson from I Corinthians is that the debate and discussion can be fruitful only if they are constantly steeped and resteeped in the atmosphere of the Chapter 13. It would be a sad diminution of our common Christian heritage if we were ever to accept, or imagine for a moment, that the greatest of these is clarity.

II Corinthians

The best American idiom is uniquely vivid. For instance 'that's the way the cookie crumbles'. The phrase is applied to a situation which turns out much less satisfactorily than you had hoped. You accept it with disappointment, ruefully, regretfully, as the way things are and are going to be. That's the way the cookie crumbles.

At the time he wrote the Second Letter to Corinth, Paul's cookie had crumbled very badly. Everything had gone wrong, disastrously wrong and Paul was near to despair, 'For we should like you to realise brothers, that the things we had to undergo in Asia were more of a burden than we could carry so that we despaired of coming through alive' (1:8).

From Asia he had crossed into Macedonia; it was out of the frying pan into the fire, 'Even after we had come to Macedonia, however, there was no rest for this body of ours. Far from it; we found trouble on all sides, quarrels outside, misgivings inside' (7:5). Later on his mind goes back over the hardship years; he recalls the endless work, the beatings, the dangers, the sleeplessness, and the hunger, 'and, to leave out much more, there is my daily preoccupation; my anxiety for all the Churches' (11:28). What made the hardships all the harder to bear was mistrust from his friends in

Corinth. They were suspicious and angry because Paul had cancelled a promised visit. He, on the other hand, was deeply hurt by them because they, just then cool towards Paul, had given welcome to 'counterfeit apostles, they are dishonest workmen, disguised as apostles of Christ' (11:13). In jail Oscar Wilde wrote a beautiful little work called *De Profundis*. The Second Letter to the Corinthians is Paul's *De Profundis* and he sums up the way he feels, 'Indeed while we are still alive, we are consigned to our death every day' (4:11). That, as Paul saw it just then, was the way the cookie crumbled.

But that is only one half of II Corinthians—the suffering, the frustration, the disappointment, in a word, the Cross. For this Letter is the letter of light and shadow, the light all the more splendid because the shadow is so deep. The crushing anguish drove Paul to meditate more profoundly on Christ and his sufferings. For Christ, Paul reflected, suffering and death were the God-appointed path to resurrection and glory. This illuminated everything. Since Christians were one with Christ, obviously they must share his suffering, and the suffering would lead them where it had already led Christ. Indeed these sufferings were already transfigured by a light that never was on sea or land and that came from the Risen Christ. What Christ had said to the Emmaus disciples was profoundly true also of the *whole* Christ, 'Was it not ordained that the Christ should suffer and so enter into his glory' (Luke 24:26).

This is the letter of couplets: light/shadow, weakness/strength, suffering/glory, death/life. Paul has hardly begun the letter when he writes,

> Blessed be the God and Father of our Lord Jesus Christ, a gentle Father and the God of all consolation, who comforts us in all our sorrows . . . as the sufferings of Christ overflow to us, so, through Christ, does our consolation overflow. . . . Yes. we were carrying our death warrant with us and it has taught us to rely not on ourselves but only on God who raises the dead to life (II Corinthians 1:3–5,9).

That double motif runs through the entire Letter. It is Paul's meditation on the sorrows, frustrations, agonies of Christian life, especially Christian ministry, all seen in the context of Christ's Death and Resurrection. Indeed, mysteriously continuing Christ's Death and Resurrection.

This means that by comparison with the earlier chapters of I Corinthians, there is less emphasis here on the Crucified Christ; more on the Risen Christ. The worries, the weakness, the disintegration were all around for anybody with eyes to see. What was hard to believe was that these *'earthenware jars'*, ourselves, could be the bearers of *'such an overwhelming power'* (4:7), that comes from God and not from ourselves. The emphasis continues, 'Even if we did once know Christ in the flesh, that is not how we know him now. And for anyone who is in Christ there is a new creation' (5:16–17). Or again, 'he was crucified through weakness, and still he lives now through the power of God' (13:4). Paul writes of himself and the other Apostles as being 'partners of his triumph' (2:14). Apparently Paul thought there was something to be said for a triumphalist Christianity: which of course is only another way of saying a Resurrection Christianity. In Chapter 3, Paul, searching for a metaphor to convey how Christ's splendour is shared with us writes, 'And we, with our unveiled faces reflecting like mirrors the brightness of the Lord, all grow brighter and brighter as we are turned into the image that we reflect; this is the work of the Lord who is Spirit' (3:18). There, for Paul, is the light transforming all the darkness, 'the light of the knowledge of God's glory, the glory on the face of Christ' (4:6).

So the Christ of II Corinthians is pre-eminently the Christ who is answer to, because he is transformer of, the human enigma of pain, frustration, disappointment and death. For the Christian, the cookie only appears to crumble. The reality is Christ taking us with him along the path of pain into his glory and his love. This, the triumph of failure, is, what this Letter is about.

Chapter VIII

CHRIST AND THE LAW

Galatians

Of the many peoples to whom Paul preached, the Galatians hold the all-time international record for making Paul angry. He cools off a bit towards the end of Galatians although his second last sentence, where normally Paul is speaking affectionate farewells, brusquely reads, 'I want no more trouble from anybody after this' (6:17). But at the beginning he is very angry indeed: angry with the senseless Galatians; with those who had tried to teach them another version of the Good News; and with Cephas who should know better, but who had behaved (in Paul's view) in a way far too open to misunderstanding. Paul is provisionally furious even with any angel who might interfere from heaven and take the wrong side of this business. He was as mad as that!

Why is Paul so angry? He tells us himself,

> Some troublemakers among you want to change the Good News of Christ; and let me warn you if anyone preaches a version of the Good News different from the one we have already preached to you, whether it be ourselves or an angel from heaven, he is to be condemned (1:7–8).

Who was trying to change the meaning of the Good News? They were Judaisers, trying to persuade the neo-Christians that, Christ or no Christ, in order to win salvation it was necessary to observe the whole Mosaic Law. In their view, Christ's coming hadn't made any real difference to the old ways. Call yourself a Christian if you like, their argument seems to have run; one sect more or less doesn't make much difference. The important thing remains what it always has been: circumcision and the observance of the Mosaic Law. They had a further argument against Paul: was he really an Apostle? After all he had never walked with the Lord; he was just an emissary of those who had and really shouldn't be taken as seriously as he was taking himself.

This view about the Mosaic Law was not new to Paul. After all it had been the central topic of the Council of Jerusalem and everywhere Paul went among the Jews of the *diaspora*, the problem confronted him: what *was* the relationship of Christ to the old Law? But in Galatia, the Christians were disposed to listen to siren voices, so an angry Paul turns on them, part invective, part pleading, always loving. The central thing he wants to say is quite clear, 'If you do look to the Law to make you justified, then you have separated yourselves from Christ . . . in Christ Jesus whether you are circumcised or not makes no difference—what matters is faith that makes its power felt through love' (Galatians 5:4–6). This is the Christ who especially appears in Galatians, the Christ who is the only source of salvation; and in whose presence the Mosaic Law, vital though it had been in its time as prelude to Christ, has now become irrelevant and, if taken as God's final word, actually destructive of the new life in Christ.

But Paul being Paul, and especially being angry, isn't content to leave it at that. In order to bring home his truth he reaches around for telling illustrations, obscurely to the Old Testament, more convincingly to current practice in the matter of making wills and educating the young. To one frame of reference he constantly returns. I dwell on this for a moment as an example of how Paul tried to enliven his teaching by presenting it in terms with which his Christians were familiar.

Galatia was a Roman province with its quota of slaves. It is easy to forget how important the institution was in the time of Paul. Scholars seem to think that over half the population may well have been slaves. Slaves could buy or win their freedom and this, though difficult, was common enough. Overwhelmingly the traffic was a one-way traffic. Slaves were anxious to become free. Free men would never freely choose to become slaves. All this was part of daily, taken-for-granted living. And it is this that Paul uses again and again throughout his Letter. Surely you are not so mad as to want to walk back into slavery again. I take a few examples.

He denounces the Judaisers, they 'have furtively crept in to spy on the liberty we enjoy in Christ Jesus and want to reduce us all to slavery' (2:4). He writes later, 'Before faith came we were allowed no freedom by the Law' (3:23) and further on in the next chapter, contrasting slaves and sons he continues, 'We were as good as slaves ... but God sent his Son, born of a woman, born a subject of the Law, to redeem the subjects of the Law and to enable us to be adopted as sons' (4:3–5). At the beginning of Chapter 5 he urges them to guard their new-found freedom, 'When Christ freed us, he meant us to remain free. Stand firm, therefore, and do not submit again to the yoke of slavery' (5:1). He returns to the metaphor some verses later in telling them about the obligations of their new freedom, 'You were called, as you know, to liberty; but be careful, or this liberty will provide an opening for self-indulgence. Serve one another, rather, in works of love' (5:13).

All this is interesting as an example of Paul's teaching methods. But it is interesting from another angle, too. Paul was nearly two thousand years ahead of his time when, in Galatians, he articulated Christian truth in a Theology of Liberation.

So the Christ of Galatians is Christ the Liberator, the one who sets us free from slavery, sin and death; Christ the Redeemer; Christ to whom, as opposed to the Mosaic Law, we must look for everything in our relations with God. *How* God sets us free through Christ is summed up in a passage just quoted: 'God sent his Son, born of a woman, born a subject of the Law, to redeem the subjects of the Law and to enable us to be adopted as sons' (4:4–5). This is a key passage from Galatians but it is much more than that. Nowhere does Paul sum up so well in a few words the kernel of his teaching. Elsewhere he spells the same message out in more expanded form, for example in Chapter 8 of Romans or the introductory prayer of Ephesians. But the essential Paul is found in these twenty-nine words from Galatians.

The redeeming, liberating Christ of Galatians is nearly always the Crucified Christ. There is only one reference (1:3) to the Risen Christ. Immediately after that Paul turns to 'the Lord Jesus Christ, who in order to rescue us from the present wicked world sacrificed himself for our sins' (1:3–4). There on Calvary his mind stays. This fixation on Calvary comes vividly through towards the end of the second chapter,

> I have been crucified with Christ, and I live now not with my own life but the life of Christ who lives in me. The life I now live in this body I live in faith: faith in the Son of God who loved me and sacrificed himself for my sake (2:9).

Just after that he looks back in anger at the fickleness of his Galatian converts, 'Are you people in Galatia mad? Has someone put a spell on you, in spite of the plain explanation you have had of the crucifixion of Jesus Christ?' (3:1.) Crucifixion, note, not Resurrection. The same emphasis is found a few verses further on, 'Christ redeemed us from the curse of the Law by being cursed for our sake, since Scripture says: "cursed be everyone who is hanged on a tree" ' (3:13). In the fifth chapter Paul writes that splendid passage about the fruits of the Spirit, giving us in a few words the atmosphere of authentic Christian life. It is a passage in which one would expect a reference to the Risen Christ and his life in us through the Spirit, but Paul automatically returns to the idiom of Calvary. 'You cannot belong to Christ Jesus unless you crucify all self-indulgent passions and desires' (5:24). In the last paragraph he searches for a phrase to describe the Judaisers and can find nothing more forceful than to call them enemies of the Cross of Christ. And finally there is that mysterious phrase at the end, 'the marks on my body are those of Jesus' (6:17).

There is no doubt that the Passion was uppermost in Paul's mind when he was writing Galatians. Later Letters, especially Colossians and Ephesians, will find Paul focused more on the glorious and Risen Christ, the image of God, the centre of creation, the Christ, if you like, of Teilhard de Chardin. But the path to that, for Paul, clearly lay along the Way of the Cross. It is a good path to follow, specially in an age only too ready to forget the Cross. That is part of the message for our times from the Letter to the Galatians.

84

Romans

It is with a feeling of near helplessness that one tries to say something of Paul's Christ as he emerges in Romans. The Letter is enormously rich, varied, comprehensive and at times very puzzling, and I expect it is true to say that amateurs jump in where scholars fear to tread. Still the original meaning of the word amateur is one who loves. That is my chief qualification for writing about Romans.

Romans and Galatians belong, of course, together. A pastoral problem in Galatia (as we have just seen) had compelled Paul to focus on the question: what exactly is the relationship between the Mosaic Law and the new Way? This in turn led to a wider question: what are the inescapable essentials if man, man anywhere, is to escape from sin and death and is to regain his heritage of filial companionship with a loving God?

Galatians contained the bones of an answer to these ultimate questions. But Galatians was chiefly pastoral guidance; hurried, angry, pastoral guidance at that. Poetry has been defined as emotion remembered in tranquillity. Romans is Galatians remembered in tranquillity. Indeed I expect that most good theology is impassioned religious debate remembered in tranquillity. Theologians nowadays sometimes tell us that orthopraxis should come before orthodoxy. In these terms Galatians is near to orthopraxis, Romans to orthodoxy. I think it of some interest, and indicative of much to come, that Christian experience and controversy should here have dictated the agenda for the beginnings of Christian Theology. For in Romans Paul is mostly theologian and Romans is faith seeking understanding.

By Paul's standards, never too high in the matter of order and sequence, Romans is an orderly letter. He puts his thesis, not exactly at the beginning—that would be too much to expect from Paul, even on an orderly day—but towards the end of the third chapter,

> God's justice that was made known through the Law and the Prophets has now been revealed outside the Law, since it is the same justice of God that comes through faith to everyone, Jew and pagan alike, who believes in Jesus Christ. Both Jew and pagan sinned and forfeited God's

glory, and both are justified through the free gift of grace by being redeemed in Christ Jesus who was appointed by God to sacrifice his life so as to win reconciliation through faith (3:21–5).

Paul's universalism comes clearly through here. This message, this salvation is for everybody; and for everybody on the same terms. But in spite of himself Paul, being a Jew, was especially interested in the Law and how *that* was related to the new life in Christ. Later on in the Letter in an affectionate passage, mourning the blindness of his fellow-Jews, he describes their basic error: 'I can swear to their fervour for God but their zeal is misguided. Failing to recognise the righteousness that comes from God, they try to promote their own idea of it . . . But now the Law has come to an end with Christ' (10:2–4). What was wrong with this Law which, for all its excellence, now hindered rather than helped? What was it about the Law that in these, the last ages, thwarted the proper relationship between man and God?

To this question scholars have given a scholarly answer; for an answer at once scholarly and yet easily readable I could refer the reader to no better source than C. H. Dodd in *The Meaning of Paul for To-day* especially in the chapter entitled 'The Tyranny of an Idea'. I cannot, of course, add to scholarship of this quality. All I *can* do is, accepting this scholarship, to seek to understand better what Paul was so deadly in earnest about and try to present it in terms perhaps more intelligible to those who, like myself, make no special claims to biblical scholarship. I believe Paul's quarrel with everything he summarised as the Law is simply the reverse side of the central doctrine he preached—our sonship of God in and with Christ.

Sons of God—that is the best description of the new relationship with God inaugurated by Christ. The best of fathers, loving the most unlovable sons, caring for them, curing them, eager freely to pour out on them not just what he has but all he is—that is how men are to conceive the new relationship. It is very much a family affair. It is almost exactly the opposite of a legal arrangement.

Indeed a legal arrangement is, almost of its nature, destructive of the family atmosphere. I take an example: as Chesterton used to say, silly examples are always simpler. Let's imagine a childless couple, long disappointed, at last having a son of their own to whom to give all their affection, the obvious inheritor of all that the parents own. But the child gives the parents a lot of pleasure too. The early smiles, the first step, the first word—all this will more than reward the parents for all they lovingly give.

But suppose—it is here the illustration turns silly—that young John Jones is an unusually precocious child. At the age of six months, let us say, he calls in his lawyers to draw up a legal arrangement with Mr Jones, Senior, and Mrs Jones. This new arrangement specifies that whereas Mr and Mrs Jones (the first party to the contract) will guarantee the aforesaid John Jones ample supplies of milk, reasonable warmth and, later on, a supply of toys to be calculated according to the national average over the previous five years, the second party to the contact, to wit John Jones, Junior, will smile regularly at his parents four times in the morning and (after his afternoon nap) five times in the evening. All very silly of course—but if possible in some 'Alice-in-Wonderland' world, the attempt to superimpose the legal arrangement on the family atmosphere would simply knock the bottom out of the family atmosphere. The approaches are incompatible.

Something like that was the way Paul saw the Law in relation to Christianity. God wanted to pour out all, even his own inner life, on all who would receive it; in John's phrase, he gave them the power to be made sons of God. All this was pure gift. Human beings could never achieve it, never merit it. They could only accept it as unmerited free gift or not at all. Again and again in Romans Paul comes back to this idea of total gratuitousness, in other words grace. For example, 'Divine grace, coming through one man, Jesus Christ, came to so many as an abundant free gift' (5:15). Two verses later, 'One man, Jesus Christ, will cause everyone to reign in life who receives the free gift he does not deserve, of being made righteous' (5:17). He reminds the Romans, 'You are living by grace and not by Law' (6:14). This aspect of total gratuity finds perhaps its most concise expression in Romans at the end of Chapter 6, 'The present given by God is eternal life in Christ Jesus Our Lord' (6:23). The present of course was sonship in the Son; all else flows from that. As Paul puts it, 'Since God did not spare his own Son but gave him up to benefit us all, we may be certain, after such a gift, that he will not refuse anything he can give' (8:32). Divine sonship, gratuitously given, incredibly shared—this gift was the essence of Paul's Good News. It was very much a family affair, at heart a matter of loving personal relationships. It was the antithesis of a legal arrangement.

The Jewish failure, as Paul presents it in Romans, was to persist in thinking in terms of a legal arrangement, 'Why did they fail? Because they relied on good deeds instead of trusting in faith' (9:32). We will do our part, seems to have been their attitude, by observing to its last detail the prescriptions of the Mosaic Law; then it's up to God to keep his part of the arrangement, to look after us, his chosen people. In a sense they were worshipping an idol, a little God who wanted to give laws rather than the real God who wanted to give love. Their picture was wrong at the centre. This threw all else out of focus and distorted the total relationship. They must come to a new world-vision, a new God-vision of the kind described towards the end of the first Christian century in the Letter to Titus,

> But when the kindness and love of God our saviour for mankind were revealed, it was not because he was concerned with any righteous action we might have done ourselves; it was for no reason except his own compassion that he saved us (Titus 3:4–5).

Or, more pithily, returning to Paul and Romans, 'The only thing that counts is not what human beings want or try to do but the mercy of God' (9:16). All that comes in Christ can be accepted as gift or rejected as gift. Gift, God's totally gratuitous gift, it always remains; in other words grace. To think of it and respond to it in terms approaching those of a legal arrangement was one way of rejecting it.

'*What human beings want or try to do*' (9:16)—if this is so unimportant as Paul suggests, is there not an implicit invitation to moral anarchy? Paul, aware of this danger, adverts to it in the opening lines of Chapter 6. 'Does it follow that we should remain in sin so as to let grace have greater scope? Of course not' (6:1). The whole question of moral behaviour comes back in, but by a side door—in a subordinate role, no longer at the centre. Paul's best expression of this new role of morality is found in Ephesians, 'I the prisoner in the Lord implore you therefore to lead a life worthy of your vocation'. 'Try then to imitate God, as children of his that he loves' (4:1 and 5:1). That is the Pauline basis of Christian morality; God's children, so richly graced and gifted, should behave in a manner worthy of their gifts. For Paul, the imperative always follows from the indicative. What we should do arises automatically from what we are.

The mistake of the Jews was that of seeing man's relationship to God primarily in terms of behaviour. I sometimes wonder if the mistake is confined to the Jews. I rather think that human nature has an incurable tendency in that direction. I expect the Christianity in which I grew up was typical. If I had been asked at, say the age of twenty, what made a good Catholic, I imagine that, like most of my contemporaries, I would have replied, 'A good Catholic is one who goes to Mass and the Sacraments and tries to keep the Commandments of God and his Church.' All true enough in a way and yet needing so badly to be set in the Pauline context, 'the only thing that counts is not what human beings want or try to do, but the mercy of God' (Romans 9:16). What we do as Christians is so much less important than what we are, and what we are is simply God's gift in love.

Like the Jews, we find it easier to concentrate on the rules. Keep them and all will be well; indeed there can be a kind of satisfaction in feeling that we have fasted twice a week and have given tithes of all we possess. But deep down in us I suspect there is a half-smothered realisation that it is a terrible thing to fall into the hands of the loving God. It is easier to worry about the by-laws.

I may seem to have digressed from the central theme of this chapter: what does Romans tell us about Paul's understanding of Christ? The digression is more apparent than real. For Romans, developing the ideas of Galatians, is centrally about sonship; it is Paul's commentary on John's fifteen-word statement that goes to the very heart of the Christian vision: 'But to all who did accept him he gave power to become children of God' (John 1:12). God's universal and unbounded mercy—one could also truthfully say that *this* is the theme of Romans—reaches out in time to 'the ones he chose specially long ago and intended to become true images of his Son, so that his Son might be the eldest of many brothers' (Romans

8:29). That is the Christ of Romans: the eternal Son, centre of the whole redemptive process—men becoming sons in the Son. Around that centre other great themes take their place: how men can respond to or refuse the offer of sonship; a new relationship of shared life between Christ and those who accept him; the role of the Holy Spirit in shaping us as sons. To these great themes I hope to return in another volume. But like a sun in Paul's sky, shining behind all, illuminating all, enriching all, ultimately giving meaning to all, is what Paul calls 'the love of God made visible in Christ Jesus our Lord' (8:39).

PART FOUR

Paul on Mission

Chapter IX

GOD'S MESSAGE
(1 THESSALONIANS 2:13)

Paul, always seeing himself as authentic messenger, also sees himself
as entrusted with an authentic message. The message he brings is
not some human concoction. It is, quite simply, God's central
message to man. Paul is its bearer, not its author. Almost as soon
as he begins to write, Paul insists on this truth, constantly to recur,
'As soon as you heard the message that we brought you as God's
message, you accepted it for what it really is, God's message and
not some human thinking' (I Thessalonians 2:13). The message he
had personally received from Christ: this is how he describes it in
reference to the Eucharist.

> For this is what I received from the Lord, and in turn passed on to you,
> that on the same night that he was betrayed, the Lord Jesus took some
> bread and thanked God for it and broke it and he said 'This is my body
> which is for you' (I Corinthians 11:23).

Since it is God's message, not man's creation, it may not be tam-
pered with or watered down, 'We do not, like so many others,
adulterate the word of God, we preach it in all its purity, as God
gave it to us, standing before God's presence in Christ' (II Corinthians 2:17. Knox). This immutability of God's message is very
much on Paul's angry mind as he begins his Letter to Galatia: no
one can dare to change God's word. 'The Good News I preached
is not a human message that I was given by men, it was something
I learned only through a revelation of Jesus Christ' (Galatians 1:11).
People, Paul foresees, will resist and even resent this unchanging

93

truth; will be more interested in what sounds new than in what remains unchangingly true. But authentic message and messenger do not bow before the changing winds of human opinion. However flexible Christianity may and should be at the edges, unless there is inflexibility at the core of the message, it is not Pauline Christianity.

*

What, as it appears in the Pauline Letters, is the unchanging core of God's message? I do not think that Paul ever set himself the task of giving a formal and full answer to that question. But it is in his mind all along the way from the short and somewhat scrappy Letters to Thessalonika; through the highly personal and warm-hearted Letters to Corinth, Galatia and Philippi and the more sober and thoughtful Letter to Rome. The great christological Letters to the Colossians and Ephesians might almost have been written in response to the question. This unchanging core is, of course, always concerned with the person of Christ, with his relationship to his Father and his relationship to mankind. But if Paul does not deal with this fully anywhere, in a sense he deals with it everywhere, here underlining this aspect of the total mystery of Christ; there, perhaps in response to a particular need, emphasising another. It seems worth while to follow Paul briefly through some of his Letters in search of the inviolable core of the message.

The first passage dealing with this occurs in his first Letter, written to Thessalonika where, apparently, most of his neo-Christians were converts from paganism. He reminds them how

> you broke with idolatry when you were converted to God and became servants of the real, living God; and how you are now waiting for Jesus, his Son, whom he raised from the dead, to come from Heaven to save us from the retribution which is coming (I Thessalonians 1:9–10).

It is hard to read the New Testament with fresh eyes. All that this passage says is so familiar that one could read it, accept it effortlessly and totally fail to realise how much Paul has packed into it. They have been converted to *reality*: now for the first time they

94

are consciously living in the only *real* world there is, God's world. At the centre of this new real world there is the real, the living God: this is in obvious contrast to the lifeless gods, the objects of their homage before the coming of the Good News. This real, living God has a Son, the man known as Jesus. God has raised this Jesus from the dead. Jesus, now at the right hand of the Father, will come (shortly?) to save us from the retribution to come. It is curious that while Paul mentions the Resurrection here there is no mention of Crucifixion. Neither is there any mention here of Old Testament prophesy and its fulfilment in Christ. Naturally. He is writing, in the main, to converts from paganism to whom the Old Testament would mean nothing. Even though, therefore, the core remains immutable, it can be variously presented to people in accordance with their capacity and understanding; and this brief passage from I Thessalonians seems to me an early venture in legitimate theological pluralism in the field of christology.

The next time Paul says something important about the core of his message is in I Corinthians,

> While the Jews demand miracles and Greeks look for wisdom, here are we preaching a crucified Christ, to the Jews an obstacle they cannot get over, to the pagans madness, but to those who have been called, whether they are Jews or Greeks, a Christ who is the power and wisdom of God. . . . The only knowledge I claimed to have was about Jesus and only about him as the crucified Christ (I Corinthians 1:22–4 and 2:2).

The contrast with First Thessalonians is obvious. There, no mention of Crucifixion, only Resurrection. Here, Crucifixion, no Resurrection. There are scholars who argue that Paul, all his life long, found it almost impossible to accept the scandal of the cross. Personally I should find this view hard to reconcile with the overall tone of Paul's Letters. Indeed, I believe that Paul came more and more to see the Crucifixion as the supreme, precious and irrefutable proof of the love of God. But Paul was a Jew, no doubt sharing at some point in his life the Jewish dream of a splendid conquering Messiah. It must have been an effort to bury the dream. Christ himself, to judge from the three temptations in the desert, had to bury something of the same dream. Perhaps we can see in this contrast between I Thessalonians and I Corinthians one phase in Paul's burial of the dream.

But this crucified Christ, this Christ of failure, Paul proclaims to be also 'a Christ who is the power and the wisdom of God' (I Corinthians 1:25). Paul goes on to speak of Christ's unique relationship to man, 'The human race has nothing to boast about to God, but you, God has made members of Christ Jesus and by God's doing he has become our wisdom and our virtue, and our holiness, and our freedom' (I Corinthians 1:30). Clearly whatever filial relationship we can have with God can be ours only in Christ. Paul returns strikingly to the central, indispensable place of Christ further on in the Letter in a phrase which sums up much of what he has to say all along the road from I Thessalonians to Ephesians, 'For the foundation, nobody can lay any other than the one which has already been laid, that is Jesus Christ' (I Corinthians 3:11). For Paul, whatever else is negotiable, this is not negotiable. Before he finishes the Letter Paul's thoughts go back to the Risen Christ as forerunner and guarantee of our Resurrection, 'But Christ has in fact been raised from the dead, the first-fruits of all who have fallen asleep' (I Corinthians 15:20). Call it balance, if you like, between Crucifixion and Resurrection or call it tension, both are there seeking a synthesis in Paul's reflections on Christ and his role in respect of his Father and mankind. The Crucifixion tells us more about our present struggles; the Resurrection tells us more about what we are to be. But both must be kept near the forefront of our Christian consciousness if we are to achieve, with Paul, an integrated view of Christ, the Way, the Truth and the Life, outside of whom no one can come to the Father.

For Paul, the Jew, the relationship of Christ to the Old Testament was of great importance. Again and again Christ is presented as fulfilment of Old Testament prophesy and promise, 'however many the promises God made, the Yes to them all is in him' (II Corinthians 1:20). And Paul is proud, as only a Jew could be proud, that Christ belongs ineradicably to the Jewish race. 'They are descended from the patriarchs and from their flesh and blood came Christ who is above all, God forever blessed' (Romans 9:5). We, to whom Christ represents the commencement of a new era can empathise with Paul when he speaks of Christ as the dawn of the New Crea-

96

tion. It is not nearly so easy for us to grasp how much it meant to Paul to see Christ as also the splendid climax of the vocation of the Jewish people. The Jewish past finding its completion and fulfilment in Christ; the Christian future finding its source and all its riches in Christ; past and future of mankind meeting, therefore, around the Cross and Resurrection of Christ, and discovering their true meaning only in Christ—that is something of the place of Christ in Paul's universe. And Paul is very much a Jew, conscious of the privileged and providential role of his own people but also of the limitations of that role, when he sums up in Romans the entire story of the commerce between God and man,

> Both Jew and pagan sinned and forfeited God's glory, and both are justified through the free gift of his grace by being redeemed in Christ Jesus who was appointed by God to sacrifice his life so as to win reconciliation through faith (Romans 3:23–5).

It is one of the most remarkable sentences in Paul as his mind sweeps across the entire panorama of salvation history and he sees, in the phrase from Colossians, 'There is only Christ; he is everything and he is in everything' (Colossians 3:11).

'*Christ everything and in everything*'—that is an admirable summary of Paul's teaching about Christ in Colossians and Ephesians. They are called the christological Letters simply because no other name will do. If one were to choose a phrase from either Letter to sum up both, the choice might well be: 'Christ among you your hope of glory' (Colossians 1:27). Christ among you before his coming in the flesh . . . because mankind, even before his appearing, could find salvation only in the cross to be. Christ among you, as a man among men, during his years of earthly pilgrimage, finding its climax 'when he made peace by his death on the cross' (Colossians 1:20). Christ, but now the Risen Christ, among you 'because you have died, and now the life you have is hidden with Christ in God. But when Christ is revealed—and he is your life—you too will be revealed in all your glory with him' (Colossians 3:3–4). And there is a genuine Pauline ring about the familiar words attributed to him in I Timothy and containing a great final affirmation of the central place of Christ. 'For there is only one God, and there is only one mediator

97

between God and mankind, himself a man, Christ Jesus, who sacrificed himself as a ransom for them all' (I Timothy 2:5–6). A genuine Pauline ring—but also an unaccustomed hint of serenity. The tumult of the quarrel between Jew and gentile and the corresponding need to treat of them apart, seem to have died down. There is just God on the one hand; the entire human race, Jew and gentile, on the other, and Christ as sole mediator between.

'One mediator between God and mankind, himself a man, Christ Jesus' (I Timothy 2:5); these words emphasise the genuine humanity of Christ. They do not speak of his divinity. This raises the question whether and in what sense Paul, in proclaiming in his certainly authentic Letters the central role of Christ, proclaims him as also divine. There will be no attempt here to answer that question. It has been faced and answered by Scripture scholars, with a necessarily minute examination of the texts in question, their grammar and syntax. An impressive treatment can be found in *Jesus Christ, God and Man* by Dr Raymond Brown. I think it is a fair summary of this scholarship to say that it leaves those of us who are not scholars reassured about our attachment to texts like that in Philippians, 'his state was divine, yet he did not cling to his equality with God' (Philippians 2:5) or to the words written to Corinth, 'God in Christ was reconciling the world to himself' (II Corinthians 5:19); or the very emphatic phrases from Colossians, 'He is the image of the unseen God, and the first-born of all creation, for in him were created all things in Heaven and on earth.' 'In his body lives the fullness of divinity' (Colossians 1:15; 2:9). But even though we can find genuine scholarship about these and similar texts reassuring, the certainties we live by cannot find their ultimate basis in whether a particular noun or definite article is in the nominative or the genitive. And Christian scholarship, when it is most authentic, points beyond its own rich possibilities to a teaching Church, aglow with the Holy Spirit, and hence enlightened to see that, whatever the limits of Paul's own perceptions, the things he and the other New Testament authors *do* say imply a Christ genuinely divine and so lead us towards the mystery of the Blessed Trinity.

But the Pauline Letters leave no doubt at all about one cardinal point: the Christian message is about Christ, so closely linked to God and man that he can be spoken of in terms of equality with

God and must be spoken of in terms of identity with man. By his life, but above all by his death and Resurrection, he has reconciled the human race to God and men to one another. This reconciliation, begun on earth, finds its continuation and its climax in a life beyond death, a life which can be described only as a sharing for ever in the Risen Life of Christ. Whatever God gives to man is given in Christ. Whatever man gives back to God can be given only in and through Christ. So from first to last the Pauline message is about Christ, uniquely Son of God, reconciling men to his Father and to one another so that, at the end of the human story, 'every tongue should acclaim Jesus Christ as Lord, to the glory of God the Father' (Philippians 2:21). To restrict Christianity to any lesser horizons, or to identify it with any enterprise having limits inside the world we experience, is, quite simply, not merely distortion but plain denial of Pauline Christianity.

Chapter X

THE DEPTHS THAT I SEE
(EPHESIANS 3:4)

Before you can adequately proclaim a message so precious and irreplaceable, you must profoundly understand it. That is another way of saying that apostolate compelled Paul to be a profound and prayerful theologian; specifically compelled him to be a missiologist. He claims, in Ephesians, a special illumination not given to the other Apostles, or at least not given in the same degree, about the unique role of Christ in salvation history, 'this special grace, not only of proclaiming to the pagans the infinite treasure of Christ, but also of explaining how the mystery is to be dispensed' (Ephesians 3:8). One is almost tempted to say, 'Naturally.' This special grace was demanded by his special vocation. It was part of the tool-kit inseparable from his call to be uniquely Apostle to the gentiles. *'Explaining how the mystery is to be dispensed'*: that is not a bad definition of missiology, in Paul's time or our own. A special meeting point with Paul the missiologist is of course his Letter to Rome, fairly described as an early Christian treatise on missiology. Towards the end of the Letter Paul, the active missionary, draws the conclusions from the principles laid down earlier by Paul, the missiologist. 'They will not believe in him unless they have heard of him, and they will not hear of him unless they get a preacher, and they will never have a preacher unless one is sent' (Romans 10:14–15). Paul the Apostle used his many-hued experience to enrich theology, and then used the enriched theology to make apostolate at once more human and more Christian. It is a pattern to be remembered.

'If you read my words you will have some idea of the depths that

100

I see in the mystery of Christ' (Ephesians 3:4). Did the depths include a special illumination enabling him, from the start, to perceive the mystery of the *whole* Christ, Head and members, Head mysteriously living in the members, members living in the Head, Head and members, therefore, sharing the same life and bound together in this intimate embrace of life?

If some glimpse of all this was *not* with Paul from the beginning of his apostolate, then in some sense he would have had a very inadequate understanding of what he brought. The scriptural evidence, 'Saul, Saul, why are you persecuting me?' (Acts 9:4) hints that some *vision* of the Mystical Body was with Paul from the beginning. Words to express it could come later. All of which suggests that the Mystical Body concept has a special relevance and richness for those continuing Paul's special vocation. I wonder if we have too often forgotten.

All this is related to another question of contemporary interest: how did Paul primarily think of the churches he set up? In the last analysis what were they? I find this an interesting question because the tide of first-century ideas about this seems to have run rather in the opposite direction to that of some recent Christian history. Twenty years ago, if asked to define the Church, most of us in my own communion would probably have replied with a definition stressing the juridical and institutional elements in the Church, perhaps ending up with obedience to the Pope. Today, asked the same question, we would give a somewhat different answer, by no means excluding the juridical or the institutional, but stressing more the idea of a Christ-centred community, united variously with him and with one another. Minds and mood have moved from the juridical to the Christ-mystery.

If the Letters to Timothy and Titus are any guide, the first-century tide went the other way. In the Letters certainly authentic, Paul thinks instinctively of the Christian community almost entirely in terms of its relationship to Christ: Christ sharing his own life with his members; the members, therefore, sharing it with one another. Here and there, almost in passing, Paul takes for granted certain juridical arrangements; people who will be in charge and by whom others will be guided. But this is almost juridical detail; earthenware jars (to use a phrase from Paul himself in relation to

101

his ministry—see II Corinthians 4:7) that hold this rich treasure.

The emphasis changes in the Letters to Timothy and Titus. In these there is much concern with structure and authority. There is, in the first place, the very special authority given to these two delegates. It is hardly exaggeration to say that they are to be gently ruthless in exercising it. There is the need to choose presiding elders very carefully indeed, to impose hands on them and to make sure that they do properly their job of guiding the flock, gently if possible, sternly if need be, along the right but rugged path. Structures, which figure only marginally in the Letters to Thessalonika, Corinth, Galatia, Rome or Philippi; which hardly appear at all in Colossians or Ephesians, predominate here. If we had *only* the Pastoral Letters, then a definition of the Church would have to be largely about structures, not unlike many of the definitions of the Church between the Council of Trent and Vatican II.

But, now as then, the need for structures exists at all only because of the Christ-mystery they serve and safeguard. The present self-vision of the Christian Church as essentially a Christ-centred community of faith, hope and love, and only incidentally and in service of this Christ-centred community a thing of structures, is a profoundly Pauline vision. 'The mystery is Christ among you, your hope of glory' (Colossians 1:27). This recaptured Pauline vision, one of the central insights of Vatican II, is an insight of which we are still only learning the profound, joyous, but sometimes painful implications. It means that while both Christ-mystery and structures must always stay with us, the structures must be judged by whether and how well they serve the Christ-mystery and not *vice versa*. It is a road of which we can see the beginning but can hardly guess the end. We are hardly meant to. 'Since the Spirit is our life, let us be directed by the Spirit' (Galatians 5:25). Or as Newman put it,

Lead kindly Light amid the encircling gloom
Lead thou me on.

*

I have looked at Paul's background as preparation for his apostolate; at Paul's own concept of what his vocation imposed; at some of the special insights into the Christ-mystery which God appears to have given Paul to fit him for his unique ministry. I turn now to a cognate question. What was it deep down inside Paul that kept him going over the rugged road and years of apostolate? You could phrase the reply to that in many different ways but all of them in the end would say the same thing. What kept Paul going was a total preoccupation with Christ.

Earlier I have tried to trace something of this, Paul's preoccupation with Christ, and suggested how the various Letters, in differing and complementary ways, give us a rich and composite picture of this preoccupation. I do not propose to explore all this again. I only draw attention to two decisive elements inside Paul's preoccupation with Christ. One was total conviction. The other was total commitment.

Total conviction: take that away and Paul's life would be insane. From Damascus where, shortly after his conversion, he 'demonstrated that Jesus was the Christ' (Acts 9:22). Paul is a man never doubting that 'there is only one God, and there is only one mediator between God and mankind, himself a man, Christ Jesus, who sacrificed himself as a ransom for them all' (I Timothy 2:5–6). Himself a man—and yet, as in II Corinthians, 'God in Christ was reconciling the world to himself' (II Corinthians 5:19); or as in Colossians, 'In his body lives the fullness of the divinity' (Colossians 2:9); or in Philippians, 'His state was divine' (Philippians 2:6). One leaves to the exegetes the question in what sense Paul speaks of Christ as divine. But to any reader this much is clear. Whenever God reaches down to man or man genuinely reaches up to God then, for Paul, Christ is at the heart of the outreach of God and the upreach of man; and both the outreach and the upreach find their meeting point at the Cross and Resurrection.

Whence this ineradicable conviction, the first element in Paul's total preoccupation with Christ? For the ultimate answer to that question, one must, no doubt, think of the Holy Spirit leading Paul also, indeed Paul especially, into all truth. But, taking for granted the Holy Spirit as the main author of what Paul calls 'our certainty in Christ' (II Corinthians 1:22. Knox), is it possible to discern from Paul's Letters where Paul's mind instinctively went in search of certainty and reassurance? In other words in search of conviction.

For me there is no doubt about the answer to that question. Paul's mind went instinctively to Christ's Resurrection. The evidence for this is found all over Paul's Letters and I look at only a few illustrations. In Corinth, for example, some Christians are saying that there is no Resurrection from the dead. To Paul this is blasphemy. If you take away *our* Resurrection, you take away also Christ's Resurrection; and if you take away Christ's Resurrection you have nothing left. 'If the dead are not raised, Christ has not been raised, and if Christ has not been raised, you are still in your sins. ... But Christ has in fact been raised from the dead' (I Corinthians 15:16–20). Paul should know. He had met, talked to, been commissioned by the Risen Christ. He is witness of the Resurrection. This, the basis he offers to the Corinthians for their faith, is in the first instance the basis for his own.

In the Letter to Ephesus he is praying that his converts there may come to understand more fully the great things God wants to do in them: things having their term in the life to come but beginning in the here-and-now. The obvious questions were, 'How do we know? How can we be sure?' Again Paul points, automatically, to the Resurrection. 'This you can tell from the strength of his power at work in Christ, when he used it to raise him from the dead' (Ephesians 1:19–20). Uncertain in Philippians whether or not he himself may quite soon be executed, his mind, searching for reassurance, goes at once to Christ's Resurrection as source and guarantee of ours, 'He will transfigure these wretched bodies of ours into copies of his own glorious body. He will do that by the same power with which he can subdue the whole universe' (Philippians 3:21). Nowhere, I think, is the central importance of the Resurrection more cogently asserted than in the second sentence of the careful treatise to the Romans where he sums up the essence of his gospel. This Good News

> is about the Son of God who, according to the human nature he took, was a descendant of David: it is about Jesus Christ our Lord who, in the order of the Spirit, the Spirit of holiness that was in him, was

proclaimed Son of God in all his power through his resurrection from the dead (Romans 1:3–4).

For conviction Paul goes consistently to Resurrection.

Is it the same for commitment, the other major element in Paul's preoccupation with Christ? Up to a point I expect the answer is yes. When Paul met his Master at Damascus and saw 'the light of the knowledge of God's glory, the glory on the face of Christ' (II Corinthians 4:6), there began an immediate commitment to Christ which can be described only in terms of love, fidelity, service. It was Paul's response to Christ's love. And where did Paul learn about Christ's love? Partly, no doubt, at Damascus; it was part of the glory he had seen in the face of the Risen Christ. And yet there are many hints in his Letters that when Paul wanted to reassure himself about the reality of God's love in Christ, his mind went instinctively not to Damascus or the Resurrection but to Calvary. It happens in II Corinthians, 'The love of Christ overwhelms us when we reflect that if one man has died for all, then all men should be dead' (II Corinthians 5:14). It surfaces with astonishment in Galatians, 'The life I now live in this body I live in faith: faith in the Son of God who loved me and sacrificed himself for my sake' (Galatians 2:20). It comes meditatively in Romans, 'It is not easy to die even for a good man . . . but what proves that God loves us is that Christ died for us while we were still sinners' (Romans 5:7–8). And Paul, a little later in Romans, has been thinking of Crucifixion at least as much as Resurrection as he breaks into his great defiant cry that 'nothing that exists, nothing still to come, not any power or height or depth, nor any created thing, can ever come between us and the love of God made visible in Christ Jesus our Lord' (Romans 8:38–9).

Paul, I believe, went to the Cross perhaps even more than to the empty tomb when he sought with all the saints to grasp the breadth and the length, the height and the depth, so that, knowing the love of Christ which is beyond all knowledge, he might be filled with the utter fullness of God. Perhaps this says something about the source of Christ-commitment in our lives too.

Chapter XI

AS GOD'S MINISTERS
(II CORINTHIANS 6:4.)

Total preoccupation with Christ: that, then, is the unchanging centre of Paul's life. Total preoccupation with Christ might seem at first sight to involve a certain isolation from people. Yet Paul's life was a people-packed life, some of them thinking of themselves as Paul's enemies, a privileged few calling themselves his close friends, a multitude from Antioch to Rome seeing in him their spiritual father, the first to bring them the Good News. But Paul did not, so to speak, divide his preoccupation, giving a certain proportion to Christ and a certain proportion to people. His preoccupation with people was part of his preoccupation with Christ, the overflow of his preoccupation with Christ. Conversely, his preoccupation with Christ involved and included a preoccupation with people. All this, no doubt, was closely related to Paul's vision of the Mystical Body. All his Christians he saw as members of Christ. Those not yet Christians he saw as invited to this same close union with Christ. As he put it himself writing to Corinth, 'You, God has made members of Christ Jesus' (I Corinthians 1:29). If God had put Christ and his members together, how could Paul think of them apart?

Preoccupation with people: that is just another name for Paul's ministry. I now turn to that ministry. How did Paul conceive of or describe it?

The first thing that Paul insists on about his ministry is that he is servant of the Gospel, not its master. 'After all, what is Apollos and what is Paul? They are servants, who brought the faith to you' (I Corinthians 3:5). Servants, further, to whom the Lord has allotted certain specific tasks: 'Even the different ways in which they brought it were assigned by the Lord. I did the planting, Apollos the watering, but God made things grow' (I Corinthians 3:5–6). A few verses later he returns to this idea of service, 'Paul, Apollos, Cephas, the world, life and death, the present and the future, all are your servants' (I Corinthians 3:22). Servants have to give an account of their service so 'People must think of us as Christ's servants, stewards entrusted with the mysteries of God. What is expected of stewards is that each one should be found worthy of his trust' (I Corinthians 4:1–2). In the Roman world a servant neglecting his duties could expect punishment and Paul sees a certain parallel with himself, 'Not that I do boast of preaching the Gospel since it is a duty that has been laid on me; I should be punished if I did not preach it!' (I Corinthians 9:16). The Second Letter to the Corinthians sounds the same note of service, 'It is not ourselves that we are preaching, but Christ Jesus as the Lord, and ourselves as your servants for Jesus' sake' (II Corinthians 4:5). He returns to this idea of apostolic servitude in Colossians when he speaks about the 'Good News, which you have heard, which has been preached to the whole human race, and of which I, Paul, have become the servant' (Colossians 1:23).

But, if service, apostolate is also immense and unspeakable privilege. Even in I Corinthians, where Paul is insistent on the concept of service, he suddenly soars in the social scale and becomes an architect, 'and laid the foundations, on which someone else is doing the building' (I Corinthians 3:10). Still writing to Corinth he tells them that 'In Christ, we speak as men of sincerity, as envoys of God' (II Corinthians 2:17). The servants and stewards are also ambassadors! In the same paragraph Paul, his mind moving to the image of a victorious general from the provinces making his grand ceremonial entry into Rome writes, 'Thanks be to God who, wherever he goes, makes us, in Christ, partners of his triumph, and through us is spreading the knowledge of himself, like a sweet smell, everywhere' (II Corinthians 2:14). Still servants, yes, but servants who are close and privileged associates of the one they serve. In Ephesians apostolate emerges incontestably as precious privilege, 'on me, least as I am of all the saints, he has bestowed this privilege, of making known to the gentiles the unfathomable riches of Christ'

107

(Ephesians 3:9. Knox). If we want in capsule form Paul's attitude to his vocation, there it is, all the more appealing because expressed in this Letter of prayer. Paul is most authentic and appealing when he is Paul at prayer.

A sense of inadequacy for apostolate: that, too, stayed constantly with him. Paul saw a huge and almost comic disproportion between the richness of the message he brought and the shabbiness of the people who brought it. He constantly warned his Christians not to judge the book by the bearer. 'We are only the earthenware jars that hold this treasure, to make it clear that such an overwhelming power comes from God and not from us' (II Corinthians 4:7). Here Paul actually sees a divine purpose in the human inadequacy. If the bearers of the message were tremendously impressive people, success might be attributed to the skill of the messenger rather than the power of the message. But as it is (Paul argues) nobody in his senses could attribute the Gospel growth to this raffish bunch of itinerant preachers. So the result *must* be due to God alone. It is difficult to exaggerate how thoroughly this idea of human inadequacy for God's work permeates Paul's mind. His earlier Letter to Corinth is full of it too.

> No, it was to shame the wise that God chose what is foolish by human reckoning, and to shame what is strong that he chose the weak by human reckoning; those whom the world thinks common and contemptible are the ones God has chosen—those who are nothing at all to show up those who are everything (I Corinthians 1:27–8).

In this passage, it is true, Paul is thinking of the wider call to Christianity rather than the call to special apostolate. But one feels sure that Paul would apply these words equally to apostolate. It is fundamental in Paul that 'the only thing that counts is not what human beings want or try to do, but the mercy of God' (Romans 9:16). Apostles are visual aids illustrating this fundamental principle—they are so obviously inadequate that their sufficiency cannot come from themselves. Or as Christ put it to Paul, 'My grace is enough for you; my power is at its best in weakness' (II Corinthians 12:9).

And yet, even though the real power of the Good News comes

from God, Paul is supremely careful that the Gospel should not be hindered by avoidable human defects in the preacher. 'We are careful not to give offence to anybody, lest we should bring discredit on our ministry; as God's ministers we must do everything to make ourselves acceptable' (II Corinthians 6:4. Knox). Paul is very sensitive to what we should call today Public Relations. So he is eager to praise if he can, prepared to blame only if he must; and there is, taking the Pauline Letters as a whole, far more praise and encouragement than there is of blame. But blunt blame there is as where, in writing to Corinth, he upbraids them for their toleration of incest, their snobbery at the Eucharistic meetings or their tendency to bring their fellow-Christians, unnecessarily, before pagan courts of law. And, of course, there is the Letter to the Galatians in which Paul, exasperated and bewildered by their behaviour, can only ask angrily if they are insane.

But Paul is far more concerned to praise. In his first Letter he tells the Thessalonians that they are 'the great example to all believers in Macedonia and Achaia . . . the news of your faith in God has spread everywhere' (I Thessalonians 1:7–8). Even in his theological treatise to the Romans, he is careful to sound the note of praise, 'Your fidelity to Christ, anyway, is famous everywhere, and that makes me very happy about you' (Romans 16:19). Writing to Philippi, he recalls how generous they have been to him at a time of need, 'In the early days of the Good News . . . no other church helped me with gifts of money' (Philippians 4:16). Even in the highly personal little Letter to Philemon Paul is careful to praise before he begins to ask, 'I hear of the love and faith which you have for the Lord Jesus and all the saints. . . . they tell me, brother, how you have put new heart into the saints' (Philemon 4–6).

In another area of some contemporary interest Paul emerges as highly sensitive to audience reaction. Today missionaries are freshly aware that when they go to other cultures or Christian communities, they receive at least as much as they bring. This, sometimes seen today as a contemporary discovery, is rather less than that. Paul, writing to Rome about AD 57, expresses himself like this, 'For I am longing to see you either to strengthen you by sharing a spiritual gift with you, or what is better, to find encouragement among you from our common faith' (Romans 1:11–12). Hardly the language of a man who feels he has all to give and little to receive. Or take the advice he offers the Christians of Colossae,

> Be tactful with those who are not Christians and be sure you make the best use of your time with them. Talk to them agreeably, and with a flavour of wit, and try to fit your answers to the needs of each one (Colossians 4:5–6).

If any contemporary missiologist has something better to say as briefly on the topic, it would be of interest to hear it.

Paul, then, was very much concerned to win friends and influence people. This can be a form of egotism. Was it so in Paul's case? I think the honest answer has to be, up to a point, yes. Paul retained the weakness, if it is a weakness, of wanting to be appreciated by those he served and loved. One doubts if it ever entirely disappears from a human being or whether he would be the better Christian for its total disappearance. So the real question is not so much whether this trait disappeared from Paul but whether the trait was subordinated to his total dedication to Christ and to people. That it was so subordinated is, I think, amply indicated by Paul's Letters and life. You could go to many places in the Letters for confirmation. I know no better place than I Corinthians, 'So though I am not a slave of any man I have made myself the slave of everyone so as to win as many as I could' (I Corinthians 9:19). Enkindled words like these, especially when taken against the background of Paul's life, are not the hollow vocabulary of Public Relations but the deeper language of dedication.

Still, the impression he made remained very important to Paul and he was especially sensitive, almost morbidly sensitive, about this in relation to money. He is determined that nobody will be able to say he is making a good thing out of apostolate. As early as AD 50 we find him writing to Thessalonika, 'Let me remind you, brothers, how hard we used to work, slaving night and day so as not to be a burden on any one of you while preaching God's Good News to you' (I Thessalonians 2:9). Some seven years later we find him writing to Corinth,

> The Lord directed that those who preach the Gospel should get their

110

living from the Gospel.' . . . Do you know what my reward is? It is this: in my preaching to offer the Good News free, and not to insist on the rights that the Gospel gives me (I Corinthians 9:14–18).

He is proud and slightly defiant about this in his Second Letter to Corinth, 'I was penniless when I visited you . . . I would not, and I will not, put any burden on you. As the truth of Christ lives in me, no one in all the country of Achaia shall silence this boast of mine' (II Corinthians 11:9–10. Knox). In Philippians he expresses his gratitude for, but still proclaims his ultimate indifference to, their financial help, 'No other church helped me with gifts of money. You were the only ones.' 'I have learned to manage on whatever I have. I know how to be poor and I know how to be rich too' (Philippians 4:15–16,11–12). Paul's abnormal sensitivity about money emerges with equal clarity in Acts. At Miletus, in the farewell sermon Luke has created, Paul insists to the elders of Ephesus, 'I have never asked anyone for money or clothes; you know for your-selves that the work I did earned enough to meet my needs and those of my companions' (Acts 20:34). All this, even if early and remarkable charter for the approach of the worker priests, is also reminder that this approach should be the exception rather than the rule. It also raises the issue whether the outlook of the mission-ary on the whole question of poverty and money needs to be different from the approach characteristic of religious life, seeing poverty as evangelical counsel to be followed. For Paul, frugal self-support seems to have little to do with an evangelical counsel. It has every-thing to do with effectiveness of apostolate and reputation of Apos-tle. Like most things in Paul, missionary poverty is people-centred.

Worth noting also is a change imposed on Paul by the inexorable if enriching years. Recall for a moment Paul's first recorded words as Apostle to the gentiles, spoken to the Jewish magician, Elymas Magos, a man defending a point of view opposed to that of Paul, 'You utter fraud, you impostor, you son of the devil, you enemy of all true religion, why don't you stop twisting the straightforward ways of the Lord?' (Acts 13:10). It is in some contrast to the advice he offers in Ephesians. 'Never have grudges against others or lose your temper, or raise your voice to anybody, or call each other names' (Ephesians 4:31). Something has mellowed Paul over the crowded years. Call it life, if you like, and no doubt that would be part of the truth. But it is not just that. Paul also could grow towards the ideal he expresses for himself in Galatians, 'I have been crucified with Christ, and I live now not with my own life but with the life of Christ who lives in me' (Galatians 2:19–20). If it is authentically life in Christ, then it must grow, under the direction of the Spirit, and 'What the Spirit brings is very different; love, joy, peace, patience, kindness, goodness, trustfulness, gentleness, and self-control' (Galatians 5:22).

Chapter XII

TO PREACH THE GOOD NEWS
(I CORINTHIANS 1:17)

Paul saw his apostolate fundamentally as an apostolate of preaching. Rather oddly distinguishing between an apostolate of Word and an apostolate of Sacrament, he tells us that 'Christ did not send me to baptise but to preach the Good News' (I Corinthians 1:17). Even in casual and passing mention he takes this for granted as the core of his apostleship, 'When I went up to Troas to preach the Good News of Christ' (II Corinthians 2:12). This is the purpose of all his far wanderings, 'otherwise we should not have reached you, as we did come all the way to you with the Gospel of Christ' (II Corinthians 10:14). This central role of preaching is articulated unmistakably in the arrangement with Peter, 'They recognised that I had been commissioned to preach the Good News to the uncircumcised just as Peter had been commissioned to preach it to the circumcised' (Galatians 2:7).

Paul was essentially in the communications business. In fact a broadcaster: his job was to broadcast the Good News. I suppose he never put it quite so trenchantly as when he was talking about something else: in this case about the prosaic question—how is an apostle to eat? 'Not that I boast of preaching the Gospel, since it is a duty which has been laid on me; I should be punished if I did not preach it!' (I Corinthians 9:16). In some parts of the USA, if dressed in clerical attire, you can find yourself addressed as Preacher. At first a little startling, it is also a reminder. It invites comparison with Paul's boast, 'I have preached Christ's Good News to the utmost of my capacity' (Romans 15:19). And it invites reflection on

113

a verse of II Timothy, 'make the preaching of the Good News your life's work, in thoroughgoing service' (II Timothy 4:5).

What did Paul preach and how did he preach it? The answer to the first of these questions is easy, 'There is only Christ, he is everything and he is in everything' (Colossians 3:11). But, from Acts and Paul's Letters, we can get, I think, clearer ideas about how Paul preached.

Here and there in Acts we have some record of the impression Paul made on his hearers. The riot in Jerusalem listened to him until he told his audience how Christ had said to him, ' "Go! I am sending you out to the pagans far away." . . . at these words they began to shout, "Rid the earth of this man! He is not fit to live " ' (Acts 22:21–2). This angry reaction was no isolated instance. Tertullus, spokesman for the Sanhedrin before the Roman governor, summed it up neatly, 'we find this man a perfect pest; he stirs up trouble among Jews the world over' (Acts 24:5). Paul could and did infuriate.

And he could terrify. Felix, Roman governor during Paul's first two years as prisoner in Caesarea, was a mixed character, eager to curry favour with the Jews, hoping also to get bribes from Paul, wherever he got that idea. He had some interest in matters religious, perhaps due to Drusilla, his Jewish wife. So he gave Paul 'a hearing on the subject of faith in Jesus Christ. But when he began to treat of righteousness, self-control and the coming Judgement, Felix took fright and said, "You may go for the present; I will send for you when I find it convenient" ' (Acts 24:25). Paul is uniquely announcer of the love of God made visible in Christ Jesus our Lord. But he will call a spade a spade and a sin a sin, all the more so in the case of the great ones of the land. His tenderness goes out a great deal more readily to the shortcomings of a runaway slave.

A little later, Festus, the new governor, his guests, King Agrippa with his wife Bernice (sister of Drusilla) and the city notables of Caesarea, trooped in one day to the audience chamber to be addressed by Paul. Luke presents Paul as beginning with his own authentic Jewish background; going on to tell them about his persecution of Christianity, his conversion, his apostolate; and then giving them the core of his doctrine. At a certain point Festus, practical man of affairs from Rome and impatient of these tribal superstitions, could take it no longer, 'Paul, you are out of your mind; all that learning of yours is driving you mad' (Acts 26:24). It certainly was driving Festus mad! Paul's rapier-like reply must have made Festus very angry indeed, 'I am not mad; I am speaking nothing but the sober truth. The King understands these matters' (Acts 26:25–6). Not all the scholars would agree, but to me it seems the most efficient squelch in the New Testament. I think the unspoken implication was, 'the King understands these matters but _you_ don't.' The cutting remark seems full of the contempt of a cultivated Jew for a religious ignoramus. To make it worse, Agrippa, by professing himself almost persuaded, seems practically to join Paul in dismissing Festus as deplorably ignorant when it came to matters of religion. Agrippa after all was a Jew of sorts and blood is thicker than water. Paul emerges from the incident as master of the quick riposte; debater superbly able to take care of himself in debate; not to be tangled with lightly.

There is another interesting point about the story. To Agrippa, with a Jewish background and a believer in the prophets, Paul makes a great deal of sense. To Festus, the gentile, Paul, even after a decade or two of preaching to the gentiles, makes no sense at all. The total bewilderment of Festus finds an interesting echo from Athens, 'Does this parrot know what he's talking about? . . . He sounds like a propagandist for some outlandish gods' (Acts 17:18). I suspect that one of Paul's lifelong crosses was not so much gentile incredulity as gentile incomprehension.

But Festus did have the Roman gift of clarity, of getting to the heart of things. Telling Agrippa about his odd prisoner, Festus had said, 'his accusers did not charge him with any of the crimes I had expected; but they had some argument or other with him about their own religion and about a dead man called Jesus whom Paul alleged to be alive' (Acts 25:18–19). If, taking it for granted that Christ was invariably the subject of Paul's preaching, you go on to ask what aspect of Christ predominated, the comment of Festus gets near the heart of the matter: a dead man called Jesus whom Paul alleged to be alive. In constantly preaching Christ, Paul, more than anything else, proclaimed the Resurrection.

This may seem in contradiction to what Paul himself has written, 'While the Jews demand miracles and the Greeks look for wisdom,

115

here are we preaching a crucified Christ . . . During my stay among you the only knowledge I claimed to have was about Jesus, and only about him as the crucified Christ' (I Corinthians 1:22 and 2:3). These are memorable and impressive words. But they have to be seen in the context of Paul's wider thought-patterns and these give the ultimate emphasis in his preaching to the Resurrection.

One obvious if ambivalent source here is the various discourses or sermons attributed to Paul in Acts. There are eight such discourses in all; you could add or subtract a few, depending on whether you regard a particular passage as discourse or Pauline interjection. I treat here as discourses his sermon in the synagogue at Antioch of Pisidia (Acts 13:17–41); the brief address at the gates of Lystra to a pagan people wishing to offer sacrifices to Paul and Barnabas (Acts 14:15–18); Paul in Athens (Acts 17:16,23–31); Paul addressing the elders of Ephesus at Miletus (Acts 20:18–35); Paul addressing the riot in Jerusalem (Acts 22:1–21); and finally three discourses of Paul during his captivity in Caesarea (Acts 23:1–5; 24:11–21; 26:1–29). Of these eight discourses, two are depicted as made to pagans; four to a mixed audience of Jews and pagans; one to an audience of Jews only; and one to a group entirely Christian.

It is hardly necessary to point out these discourses are not reportage. Indeed they are better described as Lucan compositions than Pauline discourses. In Acts, as in his gospel, Luke selects, edits and presents his material with skill, care and considerable freedom. He does so for his own purposes—theological, pastoral, liturgical or polemical—purposes not always clear. In creating these discourses in Acts, Luke, no doubt, had more in mind the needs of his readers than anything Paul actually said on a particular occasion. Still it seems likely that Luke, where possible, would have filled in the flesh and blood of his discourses around a skeleton of fact. It is hardly accident that in practically all these discourses the insistent emphasis is on the Resurrection.

There are two of these eight discourses without mention of the Resurrection. The first is at Lystra (Acts 14:15) where Paul and Barnabas, suddenly appalled by a pagan city about to offer them sacrifice, rushed into the crowd to protest that they, too, are men and that there is only one God to whom sacrifice is due. They just about managed to stop the sacrifice. It was hardly a setting in which to say, 'and by the way we came to fill you in about the Resurrection.' In the sermon to the elders of Ephesus, specific mention of the Resurrection is absent for a very different and indeed obvious reason. Christ's Resurrection and the abiding presence of the Risen Jesus in his church could simply be taken for granted. Any such meeting was a meeting around the Risen Christ. Without him there would not be any meeting at all.

In all the other discourses I have listed the Resurrection is there and normally it is crucial. Even in Athens, where paganism was as sophisticated as it was simple in Lystra, Paul has a go. It was because 'he was preaching about Jesus and the resurrection' (Acts 17:18) that some described him as a propagandist for outlandish gods. And it was when Paul talked about God raising Jesus from the dead that 'some of them burst out laughing' and others said they would discuss it again sometime. That leaves five discourses: one in Antioch of Pisidia at the beginning of his apostolate and four from Paul the prisoner, towards the end.

And first, Antioch of Pisidia. Paul has hardly started on his missionary journeys when the author of Acts gives us Paul's lengthy sermon in the synagogue there. After reviewing Jewish history and presenting Jesus as the fulfilment of Jewish promise, Paul speaks briefly of the Crucifixion in five or six lines. But he goes on at once to treat of Christ's Resurrection at roughly twice that length, delaying on it, analysing it, re-asserting it, citing three separate passages from the Jewish sacred books and seeing the Resurrection as their fulfilment. The rest of the sermon, although it does not mention the Risen Christ, is all about the role of the Risen Christ and how, through him, the justification which the Law of Moses could not give 'is offered to every believer' (Acts 13:39). It is perhaps worth noting that Paul, here in Antioch of Pisidia at the start of his missionary career and speaking to Jews, is portrayed as going to Old Testament prophesy and its fulfilment in order to persuade about Christ's Resurrection. There is no mention at all of Paul's personal experience of having met and spoken to the Risen Christ.

Towards the end of Acts we have four discourses ascribed to Paul. In the first he is addressing the Jerusalem riot; in the other three he is speaking to assorted audiences in Caesarea. In all four the Resurrection is central. Twice before the Jewish leaders he

117

presents Resurrection as the great dividing issue: 'It is for our hope in the resurrection of the dead that I am on trial. . . . It is about the resurrection of the dead that I am on trial before you today' (Acts 23:6; 24:21). There was an element of tactics in this, of course, and Paul is seen as provoking dissension among his opponents, some of them accepting, some of them rejecting, a general Resurrection. But one gets an impression of more than tactics. It was the crucial question. Paul could assert all over the Roman Empire, with impunity, that Christ had died. That was just a fact of history which nobody would query. But to assert that God had raised Jesus from the dead was a very different matter. *That* was to assert something totally unacceptable to Judaism about the limitations of the Jewish vision and the transience of the Jewish dream. It was also to assert something new and startling about the meaning and destiny of man. So we find the core of Paul's preaching in his famous rhetorical question, 'Now if Christ raised from the dead is what has been preached, how can some of you be saying that there is no resurrection of the dead?' (I Corinthians 15:12).

From Antioch of Pisidia, then to Caesarea, the key theme of Paul's preaching was Christ's Resurrection. I sometimes wonder if we find, in these Lucan discourses, a hint that the *manner* in which he preached it may have changed in its emphasis. In Antioch of Pisidia we find an insistent appeal to Old Testament prophecy and not an iota of personal experience. In the two lengthy speeches towards the end of Acts (Acts 22:1–21; 26:1–23) there is little or no reference to Old Testament prophecy. But each tells how Christ, meeting Paul at Damascus, had transformed his life. The address to the Jerusalem riot also tells of another treasured meeting with Christ, this time in the Temple, 'I fell into a trance and then I saw him' (Acts 22:17). It reads like vivid autobiography. And somehow it also sounds like *Magnificat*.

If this Lucan change of emphasis reflects a change in Paul's emphasis, too, what, I wonder, was responsible for the change from Old Testament prophecy to personal experience in Paul's proclamation of the Resurrection? Part of the answer may well be the differing nature of the audiences: in Antioch of Pisidia the synagogue was full of Jews who lived by their sacred books; later audiences were more of a mixture—Jews, Romans, all sorts. But I suggest that this may be only part of the explanation. I believe the Pauline change of emphasis I speculate about could also be closely related to a fairly common experience in the area of preaching. Most of us begin by preaching bookishly, from books, feeling perhaps that the books meaning a lot to us will mean a lot also to others. Our early preaching is not very much steeped in the experience of life, partly because we may not have very much experience of life. But later we learn, often too slowly, the wisdom of the definition that preaching is truth mediated through personality. Our preaching, while it does not ignore the books, increasingly takes its life from our personal immersion in life and becomes a reflection of our own Christian experience and enthusiasm. In a sense it becomes personal testimony to the presence and power of the Lord Jesus working in our lives. If it does not grow into something like that, it can hardly be called Christian preaching at all.

Perhaps Paul went through a comparable experience. At any rate we find him portrayed, towards the end of Acts, as presenting the Resurrection with a new emphasis. He no longer seems to say, 'Look at the promises in the Sacred Books and you can easily see Christ as their fulfilment.' Instead he is presented as saying, 'I have met the Risen Christ. I have talked to him. He has talked to me. He has transfigured my life and given me the high call to bring this Good News to you. I am witness of the Resurrection.' Paul is no longer proving things out of a book. He is proclaiming the presence and transforming power of Christ in his own life.

But the nature of these Lucan discourses means that all this can be only conjecture. And Ephesians, one of the later Letters, and certainly a safer guide to Paul's later catechesis, is full of resonances of the Old Testament. It is also, for me at any rate, uniquely rich with Paul's personal experience of the Risen Christ. Perhaps the right thing is to think of the two approaches as complementary rather than contrasting, each enriching the other and both ultimately merging into one.

*

This is closely related to another idea pervading Paul's writings: the Risen Christ intimately present to Paul in his apostolate;

uniquely present in Paul's preaching, giving life through the Holy Spirit to what Paul does and says. His words have a power and an efficacy, almost a sacramental efficacy, beyond anything that the words themselves say. 'When we brought the Good News to you, it came to you not only as words, but as power and as the Holy Spirit and as utter conviction' (I Thessalonians 1:4–5). Paul's life-long concept of preaching the Gospel is admirably captured in the very last words attributed to him on the topic, 'But the Lord stood by and gave me the power, so that through me the whole message might be proclaimed for all the pagans to hear' (II Timothy 4:17). The words of the Christian preacher, then, are not just words. They are garments of the mind, at once concealing and conveying the transforming power and presence of the Risen Christ. It is a presence differing from the Eucharistic presence. But, on its own level, it is just as real.

Paul was also very conscious of the *dangers* related to preaching. Bonhoeffer writes somewhere that there is nothing so perilous as preaching the word of God to excess. The danger of which Paul speaks most vehemently is just the opposite: that the men appointed to preach the Gospel might not preach it at all. 'It is a duty that has been laid on me; I should be punished if I did not preach it!' (I Corinthians 9:16). The RSV translates the Greek much more emphatically, 'Woe to me if I do not preach the Gospel.' The words to the elders of Miletus are worth remembering,

> I have preached to you, and instructed you both in public and in your homes, urging both Jews and Greeks to turn to God and to believe in our Lord Jesus. . . . Night and day for three years I never failed to keep you right, shedding tears over each one of you (Acts 20:20–1,31).

If those of us who are ministers of the Gospel measure ourselves against these standards, few of us are likely to come away complacent.

The second big danger in relation to preaching the Gospel is alluded to in the same sermon at Miletus, 'Even from your own ranks there will be men coming forward with a travesty of the truth on their lips' (Acts 20:30). A travesty of the truth: if Paul had a recurring nightmare this was it, all the more so because his converts seemed so ready to listen to the travesty. The nightmare surfaces with exasperation in II Corinthians,

> Any newcomer has only to proclaim a new Jesus, different from the one that we preached, or you have only to receive a new spirit, different from the one you have already received, or a new Gospel, different from the one you have already accepted—and you welcome it with open arms (II Corinthians 11:4–5).

It emerges still more angrily in Galatians,

> Not that there can be more than one Good News; it is merely that some troublemakers among you want you to change the Good News of Christ; and let me warn you that if anyone preaches a version of the Good News different from the one we have already preached to you, whether it be ourselves or an angel from heaven, he is to be condemned (Galatians 1:7–8).

The Pastoral Letters, continuing this Pauline emphasis, warn about 'certain people . . . teaching strange doctrines . . . hypocrites whose consciences are branded as with a red-hot iron' (I Timothy 1:3; 4:2); and later on say that, 'Talk of this kind corrodes like gangrene' (II Timothy 2:17). On a more positive note the Letter to Titus underlines the importance of 'a firm grasp of the unchanging message of the tradition' (Titus 1:9) and goes on to say, 'I want you to be quite uncompromising in teaching all this' (Titus 3:8). Early in his ministry Paul had angrily insisted that, in contrast to some other preachers, he would have nothing to do with 'watering down the word of God' (II Corinthians 4:2). If the Church over 2000 years has been firm and even intolerant about doctrinal orthodoxy, this would appear to be very much in the Pauline tradition.

These were the two great dangers: failure to preach and the travesty of the truth. Lesser dangers get mentioned, too. Paul raises repeatedly the motivation behind the preaching of the Gospel. Profit? He touches savagely on this topic in writing to Corinth, 'At least we do not go round offering the word of God for sale, as many other people do' (II Corinthians 2:17). Paul, in spite of all the buffetting of missionary life, managed to keep his enthusiasm. But he had few illusions.

121

And yet he could be oddly tolerant of mixed motivation in preaching the Gospel. In Philippians, for example, he wrote from jail, 'My chains, in Christ, have become famous . . . and most of the brothers have taken courage in the Lord from these chains of mine and are getting more and more daring in announcing the Message without any fear' (Philippians 1:13–14). (It is worth while to note in passing that he speaks of *'the brothers'*. Not just the elders or the presbyters; Paul appears to have taken it for granted that every Christian should be an apostle.) Why are the Christians so preaching the Gospel? Some, who proclaim 'Christ for jealous or selfish motives, do not mind if they make my chains heavier to bear' (Philippians 1:17). Paul, however, chooses to look, not at the human shadows, but at the positive side. 'But does it matter? Whether from dishonest motives or in sincerity, Christ is proclaimed; and that makes me happy' (Philippians 1:18). Not the least of the lessons to be learned from Paul is to see and rejoice in whatever is positive among the ambiguities and ambivalences of apostolate in the raw. Paul seems to have understood well the tangled skein which human motivation, even at its Christian best, normally remains. No doubt he had learned a lot about it from looking into his own heart. The ideal always remains that articulated by Paul in his treatise on Ministry, the Second Letter to Corinth, 'For it is not ourselves we are preaching, but Christ Jesus as the Lord, and ourselves as your servants for Jesus' sake' (II Corinthians 4:5). It is legitimate to wonder whether even in the case of Paul it was enunciation of an ideal rather than assertion of total achievement. But, whatever about Paul, for most of us this side of death *'to me to live is Christ'* is proclamation of direction rather than of terminus. Perhaps there is a sense in which it is better so, 'For it is when I am weak that I am strong' (II Corinthians 12:10).

Chapter XIII

PAUL OF THE CROSS

'I myself will show him how much he himself must suffer for my name' (Acts 9:16). That, practically the first thing the Risen Christ says about Paul, underlines the central place the Cross is to have in Paul's apostolate. Christ certainly kept his promise. Every second page of Acts and the Letters is stamped with the sign of the Cross.

It was a Cross that took many shapes. As early as AD 49 Paul could speak of 'God who gave us the courage to proclaim his Good News to you in the face of great opposition' (I Thessalonians 2:2). The opposition would continue and indeed intensify to a point where it was scarcely bearable, 'The things we had to undergo in Asia were more of a burden than we could carry, so that we despaired of coming through alive' (II Corinthians 1:8). This particular Letter, more than any other, tells us vividly about the place of the Cross in Paul's apostolate. In Chapter 2, he recalls the external suffering and drudgery of travel and apostolate: prison, flogging, stoning, brigands, shipwreck, rivers, sleeplessness, cold, hunger, thirst. I note in passing that Paul does not complain of heat; he must have belonged to those who revel in the sun. There was the deeper suffering that is one of the penalties of caring, 'my daily preoccupation: my anxiety for all the churches. When any man has had scruples, I have had scruples with him; when any man is made to fall, I am tortured' (II Corinthians 11:28–9). There was the mysterious unidentified suffering from which Paul asked three times to be delivered, and which he describes as a thorn in the flesh. The metaphor Paul chooses suggests a pain that was acute and continuous; a thorn in the flesh keeps reminding you of its presence. In the same paragraph Paul uses very strong language indeed, 'with insults, hardships, persecutions, and the agonies I go through for Christ's sake' (II Corinthians 12:10). All this the Second Letter to the Corinthians tells us about; but it reveals a still more lacerating wound, an open wound, in Paul's heart. It was unrequited love. 'Because I love you more, must I be loved the less?' (II Corinthians 12:15). Was it weakness in Paul? Perhaps. But it is very like the weakness of. Christ mourning over a Jerusalem that refused to return his love.

The Second Letter to the Corinthians, then, uniquely tells us about the Cross in Paul's life. But other Letters adds something too. Philippians, Ephesians and Colossians, all written from jail, remind us of Paul's long imprisonments: of what Paul calls 'my chains in Christ'. In Philippians, at least, there is the possibility of execution and, while Paul writes bravely, there runs through the Letter a barely perceptible shudder of fear. Paul can hardly get his mind away from grim possibilities. The end at least near, Paul is pictured as looking back over the road since Damascus,

> You know . . . the persecutions . . . that came to me in places like Antioch, Iconium and Lystra—all the persecutions I have endured . . . anybody who tries to live in devotion to Christ is certain to be attacked (II Timothy 3:10–12).

In Paul's own authentic phrase, 'no rest for this body of ours. Far from it; we found trouble on all sides; quarrels outside, misgivings inside' (II Corinthians 7:5).

For Paul, then, the Cross was a continuing fact of apostolate. How did he come to understand it? As always Paul went to Christ; where else was there to go? But, for a more profound understanding of the Cross in his own life and apostolate, Paul went in a special way to Calvary. His Letters chart, I believe, a certain deepening in Paul's understanding of the Crucifixion. I should like to follow him briefly along this inner journey. We find Paul's earliest reflections on Calvary in the opening chapters of I Corinthians. These first reflections are characterised by an attitude of defiance. Paul is defending the seemingly indefensible. The Jews around Corinth are expecting a Messiah, yes. But they dream of a splendid, victorious Messiah, a Messiah of splendid miracles. The gentiles, sceptical about miracles, could perhaps be interested in some new achievement of human wisdom. To both Paul defiantly offers the

> foolishness of the message we preach. . . . While the Jews demand miracles and the Greeks look for wisdom, here are we preaching a crucified Christ, to the Jews an obstacle that they cannot get over, to the pagans madness (I Corinthians 1:21–3).

Over the next few paragraphs Paul uses several words to describe Calvary: power, wisdom, strong, weak, common, contemptible, knowledge, demonstration, glory. Not once does he use a word like love. In II Corinthians the word begins to creep in, 'the love of Christ overwhelms us when we reflect that if one man has died for all . . .' (II Corinthians 5:14). Before the Letter ends, however, he is back to his earlier vocabulary, 'You have known him not as a weakling, but as a power among you. . . . he was crucified through weakness, and still he lives now through the power of God' (II Corinthians 13:3–4). So I see II Corinthians as a sort of bridge Letter, still going back (in respect of Calvary) to the understanding and vocabulary of I Corinthians, but also reaching out to the richer texture of the later Letters.

In Galatians, the Letter about Christian liberation, Paul, sounding a fresh note, appropriately begins by emphasising that the sacrifice of Christ was free, 'the Lord Jesus Christ, who in order to rescue us from this present wicked world sacrificed himself for our sins, in accordance with the will of God the Father' (Galatians 1:4–5). Sacrificed himself! This is in contrast to I Corinthians where Christ and his suffering seem to be thought of in the passive voice, e.g. 'Was it Paul that was crucified for you?'; 'the crucified Christ'; 'They would not have crucified the Lord of Glory'. Throughout the Letter to Galatia the Crucifixion is very much in Paul's mind; but now there is nothing at all about wisdom, power, strength, glory. Paul has reached a fuller understanding of Calvary and the heart of the understanding is found in one of the most familiar of all the Pauline texts, 'The life I now live in this body I live in faith: faith in the Son of God who loved me and who sacrificed himself for my sake' (Galatians 2:20). Calvary has not ceased to be the power and wisdom of God. But for an astonished and almost incredulous Paul,

125

it is becoming far more 'the love of God made visible in Christ Jesus Our Lord' (Romans 8:39). That ties up readily with Paul's initial assertion in Galatians that Christ *freely* sacrificed himself. Love is free or it is not love. The same note of freedom is, I think, the special contribution here from Philippians. Christ, in the Incarnation and Passion, is portrayed as free. He *emptied himself* and *accepted* death, death on the Cross. This is all the more striking in that, for Resurrection, Christ is immediately presented in terms more passive, 'God raised him high' (Philippians 2:9). The final shape of Paul's thought about Calvary is suggested by a tiny phrase in Ephesians, 'and follow Christ by loving as he loved you, giving himself up in our place as a fragrant offering and a sacrifice to God' (Ephesians 5:1–2). Wisdom, foolishness, strength, weakness, seem to have disappeared entirely from Paul's spontaneous vocabulary when his mind dwells on Calvary. Love says it all.

Parallel with Paul's growth in understanding Calvary there is discernible, I think, a growth in his understanding of the place of suffering in Christian life and apostolate. When Paul first speaks of suffering and persecution, it is presented simply as a fact of life, 'You, my brothers, have been like the churches of God in Christ Jesus which are in Judaea, in suffering the same treatment from your own countrymen as they have suffered from the Jews' (I Thessalonians 2:14). There is no attempt here at theological understanding, no attempt to relate the pain to the total mystery of Christ. The Paul we meet in II Corinthians is a Paul far more bruised and almost broken by suffering; but also a Paul who has learned, no doubt through suffering, to relate his pain to the Passion of Christ. 'Indeed as the sufferings of Christ overflow to us so, through Christ, does our consolation overflow' (II Corinthians 1:5). It is the first expression of an idea to recur; you could sum it up as pain-sharing with Christ. If Paul suffers, it is not just Paul who suffers but somehow it is Christ continuing to suffer in Paul. It is mysterious prolongation of the pain of Christ. Repeatedly II Corinthians returns to this theme, 'always, wherever we may be, we carry with us in our body the death of Jesus, so that the life of Jesus, too, may always be seen in our body' (II Corinthians 4:10). Later in the same Letter Paul sees the 'insults, hardships, persecutions, and the agonies I go through for Christ's sake' as creating

126

a void of human helplessness into which the onrush of divine strength can more powerfully and more lovingly come. *'For it is when I am weak that I am strong'* (II Corinthians 12:10). He ends this Letter on the same note as he began it: a sharing of pain with Christ but also a sharing of new life, 'he was crucified through weakness but still he lives now through the power of God. So then, we are weak, as he was, but we shall live with him, through the power of God' (II Corinthians 13:14).

Subsequent Letters help to fill out the picture. Galatians is remarkable for underlining the identity between Paul's pain and that of the crucified Christ,

> I have been crucified with Christ . . . the only thing I can boast about is the cross of our Lord Jesus Christ through whom the world is crucified to me, and I to the world. . . . the marks on my body are those of Jesus (Galatians 2:19; 6:14; 6:17).

All this of course must be understood in relation to the special theme of this Letter; nevertheless the insistent identification of Paul's suffering with that of Christ remains. Galatians reveals still another aspect of Paul's growth in understanding, 'You cannot belong to Christ Jesus unless you crucify all self-indulgent passions and desires' (Galatians 5:24). The real crucifixion for the Christian is now seen less in terms of the persecution without, more in terms of the struggle within. Romans continues this emphasis on the interior crucifixion, 'When he died, he died, once for all, to sin, so his life now is life with God; and in that way you too must consider yourselves to be dead to sin but alive for God in Christ Jesus' (Romans 6:10–11). Romans lets us see, too, how, just as Paul came to see Calvary primarily as love, this same concept came to dominate his understanding of Christian suffering, 'These are the trials through which we triumph, by the power of him who loved us' (Romans 8:37). Paul might agree to describe Calvary as the triumph of failure. But he would far more happily describe it as the triumph of loving. And for Paul, Christian suffering would make no sense at all apart from 'the love of God made visible in Christ Jesus our Lord' (Romans 8:39).

In Philippians the note of joy in suffering is sounded exultantly, almost triumphantly. My chains? They 'have actually been a help to the Good News' (Philippians 1:12). The persecution of the Christians in Philippi? They are being granted 'the privilege not only of believing in Christ but of suffering for him as well' (Philippians 1:29). The prospect of martyrdom? 'if my blood has to be shed . . . I shall still be happy and rejoice with all of you, and you must be just as happy and rejoice with me' (Philippians 2:17–18). Suffering then, but suffering shared with Christ and so turned into joy: such is the familiar and developing tapestry of Paul's apostolate.

But, if we are in search of a Pauline text encapsulating Paul's fullest understanding of Christian suffering, we go back, of course, to Colossians, 'It makes me happy to suffer for you, as I am suffering now, and in my own body to do what I can to make up all that has still to be undergone by Christ for the sake of his body, the Church' (Colossians 1:24).

Only forty-two words; but everything important is there. The redemptive Crucifixion of Christ when he made peace by his death on the Cross—that stands at the head of the book. Because Christ lives in Paul, and Paul in Christ, what Paul now suffers is continuation of the suffering of Calvary; without ceasing to be Paul's, it is Christ's suffering too. And since it is Christ's suffering, it continues to be redemptive for Christ's Body, the Church. The clear implication is that just as Christ's personal Crucifixion was necessary for the redemption of the world, so his continued Crucifixion in his members is somehow necessary for the salvation of the world. The Cross in apostolate is not regrettable accident or obstacle. It is as central to apostolate as Christ's Crucifixion is to redemption. It seems hardly exaggeration to say that, forever nailed with Christ to the Cross, the whole Christ redeems the whole Christ. Inside the Mystical Body, and always, of course, in total subordination to the Christ of Calvary, all Christ's members are co-redeemers.

This chapter set out to look at the place of the Cross in Paul's apostolate. Inevitably, perhaps imperceptibly, it has widened to speak also of the sufferings of Christ and the Christian community. That has been the shape of recent paragraphs simply because it is the shape of Paul's Letters. In one sense, obviously, Christ's sufferings, those of Paul, and the sufferings of the Christian community are distinct realities. But for Paul they are intermeshing realities, so closely intermeshing indeed that it is not only legitimate but imperative to describe them as a single reality. The Passion of Christ continues mysteriously among us, like Christ himself, yesterday, today and the same for ever.

It is one more reminder how Paul's master-image, that of the Mystical Body, imposes its shape on Paul's entire thought. Were it not for that, it would make no sense for Paul to write in Colossians about his sufferings completing what was wanting in the suffering of Christ. This text from Colossians guides us towards the full Pauline vision. It invites us to think of Christ, the whole Christ, mysteriously re-experiencing and repeating until the end of time the central pattern of Crucifixion and Resurrection. If with Christ we are nailed to the Cross it is only that, 'having died with Christ we shall return to life with him . . . and in that way, you too must consider yourselves to be dead to sin but alive for God in Christ Jesus' (Romans 6:8,11). In the Christian vision, Crucifixion is always for Resurrection.

That lies behind two other Pauline themes I touch on again before leaving this topic of the Cross in apostolate. At a dozen places in his Letters Paul makes it clear that, while the Christian will normally have a human reluctance to suffer, this reluctance should be anchored in a deep Christian joy, 'It makes me happy to suffer for you, as I am suffering now' (Colossians 1:24). Why not be happy? It is the familiar pattern of Emmaus, 'Was it not ordained that the Christ should suffer and so enter into his glory?' (Luke 24:26). This is closely related to another familiar theme of Paul: the transience and ludicrous unimportance of the human pain in comparison with 'the things that no eye has seen, and no ear has heard, things beyond the mind of man, all that God has prepared for those who love him' (I Corinthians 2:9). Here as everywhere, Christ is exemplar. His earthly life, when he could learn patience through suffering, lasted only some thirty-three years; his entire Passion rather less than a day; his agony on the cross some three hours. But now he is 'raised to the heights by God's right hand . . . living forever to intercede for all who come to God through him' (Acts 2:32; Hebrews 7:25). With this exemplar before him, no wonder that Paul can write, 'the troubles which are soon over, though they weigh little, train us for the carrying of a weight of eternal glory which is out of all proportion to them' (II Corinthians 4:18). And he is just as graphic when he touches on this subject in his most remarkable chapter about Sonship,

> And if we are children, we are heirs as well: heirs of God and coheirs with Christ, sharing his suffering so as to share his glory. I think that what we suffer in this life can never be compared with the glory, as yet unrevealed, which is waiting for us (Romans 8:17–18).

Still suffering, bitter while it lasts, is an inescapable element both in apostolate and Christianity. If one asks the further question, why should there be suffering at all, in Christ, in his members or indeed in anything, it is a question as deep and baffling as can be asked about our Christian faith. One doubts if anybody has the full answer to it this side of eternity. Paul does not explicitly try to answer the question. But if one were to try to frame some sort of answer based on the Pauline Letters it might go like this: In a world scarred by sin which, in alienating men from God and from one another, seeks to drive love out, suffering somehow becomes the everyday language of loving. Even Christ had to learn it when he joined us in our broken land of exile. We too know the language. But we shall not need it when we go home.

PART FIVE

Questions Today

Chapter XIV

IS AND OUGHT

Paul, pioneer in so many areas of Christian life, was pioneer also in translating the Christian *is* into the Christian *ought*. Pioneer, in other words, in moral theology. This translation of the Christian *is* into the *ought*, a task begun of course by Christ himself, always remains an unfinished business. For while the basics of Christian morality do not change, they need to be reinterpreted and re-expressed in each new age, and also in terms of the cultures and assumptions of those to whom the Gospel is preached. To import neat to Africa, Asia or Oceania a moral theology assembled in Europe is rather like importing a Mercedes to some unexplored island without enquiring whether the roads there are suitable for a Mercedes or indeed whether there are roads at all. In this recurring, everyday task of translating *is* into *ought*, does Paul offer any useful guidelines?

I think he does. I believe that some of the more important guidelines can be best illustrated by concentrating on just one moral question Paul had to face. The whole matter of foods, whether foods forbidden by Jewish tradition or offered in sacrifice to idols: what was the duty of the Christian in respect of these? This was a question not of Paul's choosing. It was put to him by the daily reality of life in places as far apart as Corinth, Rome and Colossae. It seems to have been a specially acute question in Corinth: no less than three times he returns to it in the First Letter to the Corinthians. Also apparently in Rome, for Paul deals with it at considerable length in Romans. There is a briefer reference in Colossians, and the question is still a live one in the First Letter to Timothy. Even if it now seems a peripheral question, it was real and widespread then and very much on people's minds. If you wanted a rough counterpart today, you might think of contraception. Incidentally, the question of food offered to pagan idols can still be a real question. I have found missionaries of my own Society wrestling with it in Burma.

What was Paul's answer? Or rather what were the principles behind his answer? For it is these principles, rather than the precise answer to an ephemeral question, which are likely to be of enduring value.

For his first principle Paul goes back to the first page of Genesis, 'God saw all he had made, and indeed it was very good' (Genesis 1:31). Paul says it in different ways; but it is at the heart of all his answers to the food question. When he first broaches the subject to the Corinthians, he says only, 'For me there are no forbidden things; maybe, but not everything does good' (I Corinthians 6:12). A few chapters later, and speaking specifically about food offered to idols, he begins by pointing out that, idols having no real existence, God's good gifts are not sullied by being offered to a figment of man's imagination, 'there is no god but the One. . . . there is one God, the Father, from whom all things come and for whom we exist; and there is one Lord, Jesus Christ, through whom all things come and through whom we exist' (I Corinthians 8:4,6). God's gifts remain God's gifts, and therefore good, in spite of the odd antics of man. Still on this subject of meat offered to idols, and for sale in butchers' shops, Paul reaffirms this same basic truth, 'there is no need to raise questions of conscience; for the earth and everything that is in it belong to the Lord. . . . If I take my share with thankfulness, why should I be blamed for food for which I have thanked God' (I Corinthians 10:25,30). He says much the same thing to the Romans, 'Now I am perfectly aware, of course, and I speak for the Lord Jesus, that no food is unclean in itself' (Romans 14:14). This fundamental Pauline principle is restated by the author of I Timothy.

> they will say that marriage is forbidden, and lay down rules about abstaining from foods which God created to be accepted with thanksgiving . . . Everything God has created is good, and no food is to be rejected, provided grace is said for it: the word of God and the prayer make it holy (I Timothy 4:3–5).

134

To us it sounds obvious and tame. But at the time? One need only compare Paul's teaching to the decision of James 'not to saddle you with any burden beyond these essentials: you are to abstain from food sacrificed to idols, from blood, from the meat of strangled animals, and from fornication' (Acts 15:29). Fornication comes last on the list and reads least. The contrast between Paul's approach to foods and that of James says something about the development of doctrine and Paul's role as controversial pioneer in moral theology.

For his first principle then Paul goes to the origins of Judaism. For his second principle he goes straight to the heart of Christianity. Christianity is about loving and loving is other-centred, not self-centred. Christian morality, therefore, must be other-centred too. So Paul, having laid down the principle that all foods are good, does not go on to say that a Christian may therefore eat what foods he likes, when he likes. 'Only be careful that you do not make use of this freedom in a way that proves a pitfall for the weak' (I Corinthians 8:9). Settling down to cases, he visualises one Christian, a man with a timorous conscience, seeing another Christian with a saner and broader view unconcernedly eating in a pagan temple food which had been offered to idols. The more timorous man may well be horrified, may even imitate, in bad conscience, his more emancipated fellow-Christian and so sin. 'In this way your knowledge could become the ruin of someone weak, of a brother for whom Christ died' (I Corinthians 8:11). That becomes the acid test. Will it help—or hurt—a brother for whom Christ died? Even though all things and all foods are good, it is people that matter.

Paul returns to this so insistently that it must be seen as central to his thinking about morality. Later in this same Letter to Corinth he writes,

Nobody should be looking for his own advantage, but everybody for the other man's. . . . But if someone says to you, 'this food was offered in sacrifice,' then out of consideration for the man that told you, you should not eat it (I Corinthians 10:24,28).

Romans gives the same emphasis,

135

though no food is unclean in itself . . . if your attitude towards food is upsetting your brother, then you are hardly being guided by charity. You are certainly not free to eat what you like if that means the downfall of someone for whom Christ died. . . . The best course is to abstain from meat and wine and anything else that would make your brother trip or fall or weaken in any way (Romans 14:14,15,21).

All this emphasis on people as the touchstone of Christian morality does not, of course, in Paul's case make it a human thing where God is almost irrelevant. In the Pauline vision, if you want to know *why* the commandments ultimately bind, you have to look humbly and lovingly towards God. But if you want to know just *what* the commandments are, you have also to look long and searchingly towards man.

What, then, does Paul teach us about translating the Christian *is* into the Christian *ought*, in terms of a particular culture? His first principle, for which he goes back to Genesis, suggests that in our moral perplexities we should go back with greater confidence to the basics than to the rule-books. The rule-books, however excellent, are often too heavily thumb-stained by the countries and centuries to which they belong. It is usually easier to look up the rule-books. It is harder to do what Paul did: to ask the more demanding and perhaps disturbing question. At this time, in this place, at this stage of development, what does Christian belief demand by way of Christian behaviour? This wider question includes another important question: what level, standards and norms of morality are humanly possible in this particular set of circumstances? To raise and answer these questions is hardly a recipe for a quiet life in the Church. Paul seems to have been vastly uninterested in a quiet life.

The second important lesson Paul teaches is that morality is about people. The crucial question is: does this or that line of conduct enrich people or diminish them? This, far from lessening the place of God, puts it in its only worthy setting. For it is God who above all wants to enrich people. That is why he made and redeemed them. What gets notably in the way of that enrichment is obstructive, for that reason forbidden, and we label it sinful. All that promotes the genuine enrichment of people is in accordance with God's loving design and therefore good. This principle of

136

enrichment/diminishment may be of little use as handy immediate moral guide for the perplexed Christian. But if the rule-book is not based on the principle of enrichment/diminishment, then it is not a Christian rule-book.

Paul as moralist, then, offers two main principles. In search of moral guidelines, think less of the rule-book, more of the central truths and their behavioural implications. And, day in, day out (or as Paul might put it, in season and out of season), continue insistently to ask the question: does this or that command or prohibition enrich or diminish people. In moral theology today there is a swing away from rules for rules' sake to rules for people's sake. This is very much in the tradition of Paul.

Chapter XV

OF PROPER SOWING

I move from individual morality to social morality in search of further moral guidelines Paul may offer. Paul touches on various aspects of social morality: relationships inside the home; respect for lawful authority; the obligation to pay taxes. But just as I focused on foods earlier, I focus here on the great social evil of Paul's time, slavery.

Whether Paul recognised it as the great social evil of his time is a good question. Inside the Roman Empire it was a huge inescapable fact of life, largely the basis of the economy. Some competent authorities guess that three out of every four were slaves. It was probably as difficult for Paul or his contemporaries to imagine the Roman Empire without slavery as for us to imagine our industrial society without industrial workers. And while slavery was seldom pleasant, the conditions of slavery varied enormously from the intolerable to the fairly humane. But whether Paul saw it as huge social evil, inescapable fact of life or somewhere between, the plain fact is that he did not in any immediate way crusade against slavery.

There were several obvious reasons for this, all of them duly noted by scholars, needing only a brief mention. There was the question raised a moment ago: was even Paul able to enlarge his imagination so as to visualise a world without slavery? Even if Paul could so dream, there was the hopelessness of it, a hopelessness heavily underlined by recent and remembered history. There had been several revolts of the slaves, memorably that of Spartacus. The result had been civil war, carnage of the slaves, the surviving slaves hardly better off and in many cases probably worse. There was also Paul's expectation, or at least hope, a hope dwindling with the decades, that the Second Coming of Christ was quite near. If the Second Coming was only around the corner, what was the point in uncertain efforts at profound social change? Besides, if the Christian sect, already under official suspicion, became associated in the Roman mind with a new revolt of the slaves, persecution, never long absent, would certainly intensify and those to suffer most would be the slaves, the Christian slaves worst of all.

These, no doubt, were some of the reasons in Paul's mind as he formulated his attitude towards slavery. You could sum up his short-term policy in a couple of words: make the best of a bad situation. Writing to Corinth, he deals with the basic question: should a Christian slave seek freedom? 'If, when you were called, you were a slave, do not let this bother you; but if you should have the chance of being free, accept it' (I Corinthians 7:21). It is a clear direction in favour of the *status quo*. Paul goes on immediately to say that being slave or free makes no difference in the only important thing: relationship to the Lord so 'Each one of you, my brothers, should stay as he was before God at the time of his call' (I Corinthians 7:24). Paul returns to the subject in Ephesians (6:5–9); Colossians (3:22–5); it is treated also in I Timothy (6:1–2) and Titus (2:9–10). These passages, accepting the brute fact that the vast majority of Christian slaves will live and die in slavery, tell them how to make the Christian most of their servitude. Ephesians puts in a sentence the heart of Paul's instructions, 'Work hard and willingly, but do it for the sake of the Lord and not for the sake of men' (Ephesians 6:7). But these Pauline passages are not simply an Owner's Manual. In all the authentic Letters Paul has instructions for the slave-owners too. Ephesians sums it up, 'And those of you who are employers . . . do without threats, remembering that you and they have the same Master in heaven and he is not impressed by one person more than by another' (Ephesians 6:9). If one were to sum up Paul on slavery on the basis of *these* texts from I Corinthians, Ephesians and Colossians, the summary might run: accept slavery as a continuing fact of life; make the Christian best of it, the slaves by being good slaves, the owners by being good masters; slaves and masters both accepting that in terms of Christian worth, being slave or master is an irrelevant consideration.

All this has led to one view about missionary strategy, a view

139

voiced more confidently some decades ago than today. Roughly it ran like this: Slavery was a huge social injustice, rampant all over the Roman world that was the scene of Paul's preaching. Paul never fulminated or crusaded against it. Instead he went on preaching his religious message and left the extermination of social disorder to others. Indeed, up to a point, he condoned the institution of slavery and taught both slaves and masters how to lead good Christian lives inside the structures of slavery. The missionary should imitate Paul in this policy. He may encounter grave social or political injustices. These, however, are not his special concern. He should get on with his job, a religious job, that of preaching the Gospel.

It is of course impossible to hold this view today. Authentic direction has made it clear that justice, including social justice, is a constituent part of preaching the Gospel. But even before this clear direction, was this an authentic interpretation of Paul's outlook? For me, at any rate, the answer has to be 'No'. The view in question, even though appearing to find some support in the Pauline Letters, misses the larger picture.

In the first place, Paul had only one life to live. If any man gives all his life to, say, medical research, he will make no serious contribution to the development of law. Paul's life was limited too. He couldn't do or even attempt everything. He had been given a special job to do. He describes it himself in I Corinthians as that of announcer (I Corinthians 9:27). Paul conceived his mission as that of announcing the Good News where it had not been announced before; of setting up sketchy structures in the new Christian communities, and then moving on. Even allowing for considerable stays, sometimes enforced stays, in Corinth, Rome or Ephesus, Paul was by vocation, and probably also by temperament, a man in a hurry. It was for other people, and indeed other generations, to work out the full social implications. Add to this the various factors already referred to: the omnipresence and the apparent indestructibility of slavery, the hopelessness of revolting against it, the danger to slaves in any revolt, the special danger to Christian slaves if they were perceived as leaders of a new revolt. All these were circumstances peculiar to Paul's time, arguably justifying him in a muted approach to the issue of slavery, but not to be assumed as present and justifying a muted approach to social abuses of another day. Paul's relative silence may have been golden in his special circumstances. But he would heartily have echoed the Old Testament admonition that there is a time to speak.

Indeed, in his own way and in a manner far more effective in the long run than violent and therefore probably ephemeral condemnation, Paul did speak. Side by side with his pastoral directives to slaves in Corinth, Rome or Colossae, we find Paul enunciating Christian principles which, whether he recognised it or not, were dynamite laid under the foundations of slavery. We meet it, for example, in Galatians, *the* Letter of all Paul's Letters where slavery and liberation are omnipresent background to his thinking. 'All baptised in Christ . . . there are no more distinctions between Jew and Greek, slave and free, male and female, but you are all one in Christ Jesus' (Galatians 3:27,28). You get practically the same words, certainly the same thought in Colossians, 'There is no room for distinction between Greek and Jew, between the circumcised or the uncircumcised, or between barbarian and Scythian, slave and free man. There is only Christ; he is everything and he is in everything' (Colossians 3:11). Paul's only surviving personal Letter, that to Philemon about the runaway slave, Onesimus, gives us a valuable glimpse into Paul's heart and also into his ideas about the relationship between Christian slaves and their Christian masters,

> but it was only so that you could have him back for ever, not as a slave any more, but something much better than a slave, a dear brother, especially dear to me, but how much more to you, as a blood-brother as well as a brother in the Lord (Philemon 15,16).

No distinction between slave and freeman! A slave and a dear brother! A man could not go all over the Roman world sowing ideas like that and still be described as indifferent to slavery. Either these ideas would disappear or slavery would disappear. It was slavery that disappeared. Paul had helped to lay the dynamite even though the time-fuse was long. In retrospect, I suggest, we should see the instructions to slaves in Corinth, Colossae and Ephesus as short-term pastoral directives relating Christian living to immediate reality. Onesimus is pastoral practice. But the passages just quoted from Galatians and Ephesians are not pastoral directives or prac-

141

tice. They are Pauline theology. And in the Christian world there is, in the long run, nothing so explosive as good theology.

I doubt, therefore, if a Christian apostle preaching a highly spiritualised religious message, more or less ignoring social evils and leaving these to others, can authentically claim Paul as model. To be acutely aware of social injustice and disorder, to recognise this as obstacle to the total liberation of man, and to do all that can be done by Christian methods and by an appointed herald of Christian truth to remove the injustice—that seems to me far more in the Pauline mould than to preach a disembodied Christianity, unrelated to the actual human condition.

Most Christians accept this today. And it is, of course, only the starting point for further, emphatic and sometimes violent disagreement. The angry questions swarm. Can you preach Christian truth to the hungry? Do you put most of your effort into Word and Sacrament or begin by caring for Christ in your wounded and oppressed brother? Can you really be one with the poor of the world without joining in their struggle, and even in some sense in their hatred of the rich? If at the moment Marxism is the only hope of the deprived, is it not a Christian duty to help the poor towards the one hope they have, halfway house only though it be to a more just and Christian world? If as a Christian apostle you give most of your energies to relieving the human misery of people, can you rightly call yourself a Christian apostle at all? These are some of the questions of today. Happily, the impassioned debate goes on. Happily—because the passion of the debate is reminder of the earnestness of the Christian participants. You do not get that kind of passion among the purveyors of harmless bromides.

If I have listed some of the current questions, it is not with any intention of trying to answer them. My scope is more modest. Here I raise only the question whether one can usefully look to Paul for some missionary concepts or principles relevant to the debates of today. I think we can. The first point is that Paul's apostolate was full of polemic. Paul contributed perhaps more than his share to the polemic. The polemic was most often in relation to Jews opposing or diluting Christianity but it was at once wider and more intimate than that. Some of it, at least, was in relation to his fellow-Apostles. There was the basic and smouldering question: could Paul properly be called an Apostle? There was the row with Peter in Antioch about the true meaning of the Good News. There was Paul's rejection of John Mark and the ensuing bitter row with Barnabas. So Paul's life suggests that passionate disagreement about the meaning and methods of apostolate is a perfectly normal climate for the work of preaching the Gospel. As on the Lake of Galilee, storms are quite likely to spring up suddenly, to blow hard and to rock considerably a boat in which Christ sometimes appears to be asleep.

Paul also puts us on our guard against what I see as one considerable danger today: the temptation to succumb to the dilemma of stark choice. We are frequently urged to choose between extremes: a ministry of Word and Sacrament or a ministry of helping; a caring for the poor and a concern for the rich; an earthbound Gospel and a Gospel which hardly seems to touch our earth at all. Paul's example suggests that, declining the dilemma of stark choice, we should often choose both. I believe the hardest and most necessary courage today is the courage to walk serenely down the centre, listening sympathetically to but not deflected by the groans that come from the right or the taunts from the left; but of course the question remains, where is the centre? Paul achieved an enviable balance. He spent his apostolic life scurrying over the Roman world preaching 'Jesus Christ risen from the dead, sprung from the race of David' (II Timothy 2:8). But he has also left on record his lifelong ministry to the poor and oppressed: the only thing the other Apostles 'insisted on was that we should remember to help the poor, as indeed I was anxious to do' (Galatians 2:10). Paul has something to teach us here. I doubt if he would have reacted sympathetically to the suggestion that the Apostle cannot preach the Good News to the poor and oppressed until they are liberated from their oppression. He spent a lot of his life preaching the Good News to the poorest and most oppressed of all: the slaves. If he had delayed preaching Christ, Crucified and Risen, to the slaves until the institution of slavery would have been abolished, he would never have preached Christ to them at all.

Many missionaries work today in underdeveloped countries where Marxism is always present and to many, seeing Marx as prophet of a more just social order, attractive. Not a few Christian missionaries, appalled by the social injustice they encounter and seeing other efforts at alleviation as palliative, not remedy, are attracted to Marxism too. Whether these are clutching tragically at a philosophy about to be relegated to Limbo by contemporary thinkers is a question to which nobody yet knows the answer. In a sense this somewhat theoretical question is irrelevant. On the ground, Marxism and Marx are there, repelling some, attracting many, indisputably factors in the understanding and shaping of society. Like slavery for Paul, Marxism is a fact of life, and cannot be ignored by the missionary unless he chooses to ignore reality. The question arises whether, in this matter, the missionary today has something to learn from the Pauline vision. This is uncertain country, where there are few obvious answers. But one can attempt some guess at Paul's attitude to Marxism were he preaching the Good News today in the slum cities of Asia, Africa or Latin America.

It is possible, I think, to draw a certain useful analogy with Paul's attitude towards food offered to idols. His principle there was that God had made all foods, so all foods were good. The idols to whom they had been offered didn't exist; and the foods remained uncontaminated by being offered to non-existent gods. I believe Paul might look on Karl Marx and his analysis of society in rather similar terms. Marx's brilliant mind was God's gift. True, it had been offered to what Paul would see as a non-existent god, to an idol as unreal ultimately as Diana of the Ephesians. Still, even though offered to an unreal god, Marx's mind remained a brilliant God-given mind, offering a uniquely important analysis of the ills of contemporary society. True, this analysis has all sorts of atheistic presuppositions which Paul would reject as a form of idolatry. True also that it might be very difficult to separate the idolatrous presuppositions from the brilliant analysis. Still, whatever remained true in the analysis was ultimately God's gift and in some sense God's creation. As in Genesis, God could look again at this segment of his creation and see that it was very good. So I think Paul would look critically, searchingly and sympathetically at Marxism. Critically, because Paul, whose first loyalty was to truth, could never accept 'some secondhand, empty, rational philosophy based on the principles of this world instead of on Christ' (Colossians 2:8). But also searchingly and sympathetically, hoping to learn from this brilliant mind, God's gift not only to Marx but to humanity, truths and insights helping us to understand and transform the world of human relationships. As Paul put it in Romans, 'We know that by turning everything to their good, God co-operates with all those who love him' (Romans 8:28). Everything! That includes Marxism and Marx too. And I like to think of these two great Jewish dreamers, Paul of Tarsus and Karl Marx, alike in so many ways, meeting at the end of the journey and talking to each other, as if either would listen, about the grandeur and the limitations of their two disparate dreams.

Paul, then, might well accept Marx as one useful guide helping mankind to isolate and understand the scars inflicted by social injustice on a world redeemed by Christ and in process of being transformed by the Risen Christ. Paul would also accept Marx as having a role to play in that transformation. But—and here one leaves the area of conjecture for certainty—even if Paul might accept Marx as *acolyte* to Christ, he would never for one moment accept Marx or any other as *substitute* for Christ. If there are Christian missionaries who, in practice at least, accept some such substitution, they cannot look to Paul,

> Not that there can be more than one Good News; it is merely that some troublemakers among you want to change the Good News of Christ . . . if anyone preaches a version of the Good News different from the one we have already preached to you, whether it be ourselves or an angel from heaven, he is to be condemned (Galatians 1:7–8).

And the Good News, as understood by those very close to Paul, tells, 'there is only one God and there is only one mediator between God and mankind, himself a man, Christ Jesus, who sacrificed himself as a ransom for them all' (I Timothy 2:5–6). Paul, in the first century or the twentieth, would angrily reject anything, that is dilution or diminution of that.

With equal vigour Paul would reject any attempt to equate Christ's redeeming work with any conceivable Utopia existing this side of death and Resurrection. It is true that, here on earth, we begin to share in Christ's Risen Life and this sharing should lead to a profound transformation also of our present human relationships and social structures. But to suggest that Paul's dream for humanity, risen with Christ, is fully or even mainly achievable here on the earth we know is not just misunderstanding of Paul. It is flat denial. The evidence is everywhere in the Pauline Letters. Paul, indisputably, is speaking of human destiny when he writes to Corinth,

> when the tent that we live in on earth is folded up, there is a house built by God for us, an everlasting home not made by human hands, in the heavens. . . . This is the purpose for which God made us, and he has given us the pledge of the Spirit (II Corinthians 5:1–5).

He speaks just as clearly, contrasting the passing things of earth with the abiding things of eternity, in his Letter to Philippi,

> The things they think important are earthly things. For us, our homeland is in heaven, and from heaven comes the Saviour we are waiting for, the Lord Jesus Christ, and he will transfigure these wretched bodies of ours into copies of his own glorious body (Philippians 3:19–21).

If human language means anything, Paul is speaking of a world beyond the world we know.

And yet the world we know is ours, not just to hoard but to transform. This is especially true of the world of human relationships. A world built up around Chapter 13 of I Corinthians would be unrecognisably different from the world of grasp and greed that we know and, indeed, that we are. To change one into the other, especially to change it in ourselves, is our Christian responsibility. In attempting it, Christians will, of course, be primarily guided and strengthened by Christ's New Commandment to love one another as he has loved us. But if you translate that into the grimy language of everyday sustenance, the translation might not differ all that much from, '*From each according to his capacity, to each according to his needs*'.

There is one final way in which Paul and Marx resemble each other and in which both may have something to teach us. Paul, even though he never crusaded against slavery, contributed more than most to the abolition of slavery. He did it by preaching fun-

146

damental ideas incompatible with slavery. But it was a slow process and Paul could see no results in his lifetime. When he died, perhaps around AD 67 or 68 slavery seemed as strong, as impregnable and as enduring as ever. And yet slavery was doomed. Paul's fundamental Christian ideas, gradually permeating society and gnawing at the institution of slavery from within, played no small part in its collapse. There is something similar in the story of Karl Marx. In Germany and France, as later in England, he planned and plotted, it is true, for the overthrow of a capitalist society. So did a hundred other like-minded revolutionaries, whose names are hardly remembered and whose contribution to the birth of a Marxist half-world is recognised as not specially significant. But Marx is different. Why? Chiefly because, like Paul, he became a sower of fundamental ideas. He wrote *Das Kapital*. The first volume was published in 1867. It was some fifty years later, long after the death of Marx, that a state was established incorporating the ideas of *Das Kapital*. There was a lapse of half a century between the sowing of the ideas and their incarnation in Soviet society. From Moscow the social revolution spread through the world. Paul and Marx did more to reshape society by spreading fundamental ideas than either could have done by other methods, more obviously, more immediately, and more attractively revolutionary.

These two examples raise a question for the Christian apostle, often appalled by glaring social injustice and wondering what to do. Where does his most important contribution lie? Does it lie in an apostolate of protest, confrontation and immediate impact? An understandable sense of urgency may often seem to point in that direction. For some temperaments, too, immediate and active involvement may well be more satisfying; and results, whether of outrage or appreciation, will be more immediately observable. But the case histories of Paul and Marx at least invite reflection on whether the apostolate of immediate involvement and impact is the important contribution that the apostle can make. Perhaps his unique contribution is more like that suggested by the experience of Marx and Paul: simply to continue, day in, day out, if on a humbler scale than Paul or Marx, to be Apostle, herald and teacher of basic Christian ideas incompatible with social injustice. Human rights must become increasingly important in the daily catechesis.

As in the case of Paul or Marx, the time-lag will be considerable. Basic ideas take time to germinate into social reconstruction. Perceptible impact will be minimal. There will be none of the excitement or glamour of being part of a stirring revolution. The British Museum was far from the barricades and there was little glamour in going in there day after day to write *Das Kapital*. Still, ranking with the Bible and the Koran, it has done an enormous amount to reshape our world. Banners and marching do have their place in social revolution, but in the long run it is ideas that alter the shape of society.

Perhaps one of the missionary temptations today is to be men and women in a hurry, failing to recognise that the truth we bear is too precious to be assessed in terms of immediate social impact. Perhaps we have something to learn from the lines T. S. Eliot places on the lips of Christ,

> All men are ready to invest their money
> But most expect dividends.
> I say to you: Make perfect your will.
> I say: Take no thought of the harvest
> But only of proper sowing (Choruses from *The Rock*).

Chapter XVI

THAT LOVER PAUL

At Cana of Galilee the good wine was kept to the last. By far the most important thing about Paul the Apostle still remains to be said, however inadequately one may say it. Catherine of Siena summed it up admirably when she spoke of *'That lover Paul'*. Paul was many things: traveller, teacher, controversalist, organiser, collector, writer, near-poet, miracle-worker and mystic. But through all, above all and uniting all, Paul the Apostle was Paul the lover. On an earlier page I have tried to say something about Paul's love for Christ. Here I speak rather of Paul's love for his people.

Paul might well have been giving a preview of his entire apostolate when he wrote in the first of his Letters,

> Like a mother feeding and looking after her own children, we feel so devoted and protective towards you, and had come to love you so much, that we were eager to hand over to you not only the Good News but our whole life as well (I Thessalonians 2:7–8).

Towards the end of the Letter he writes with typical Pauline audacity, 'May the Lord be generous in increasing your love and make you love one another and the whole human race as much as we love you' (I Thessalonians 3:12). Paul actually sets himself up, unashamedly, as a model of what Christian love should be! It is an audacity that stays. Writing to Corinth, he dares to say, 'Take me for your model, as I take Christ' (I Corinthians 11:1). He is still more explicit writing to the Philippians, 'God knows how much I miss you all, loving you as Christ Jesus loves you' (Philippians 1:8). As Jesus Christ loves you! It is quite a claim. And the writer of II

149

Timothy is, clearly, treasuring, perhaps also recalling, God's gifts to Paul when he writes, 'God's gift was not a spirit of timidity, but the Spirit of power, of love, and self-control' (II Timothy 1:7). Especially a gift of love. Otherwise how could any human being, even Paul, claim to love his people with (as the Knox version puts it) the tenderness of Jesus Christ himself?

This, Paul's love for his people, was far from being an impersonal, disembodied thing. It was a warm human love. Paul's repeated reference to his tears is a reminder how human. Writing to Corinth, he could tell them how an earlier Letter to them, a reproving Letter, had been written in 'deep distress and anguish of mind, and in tears' (II Corinthians 2:4). Speaking of wayward Christians, straying from the right path, he tells the Philippians, 'I have told you often, and I repeat it today with tears, there are many who are behaving as enemies of the cross of Christ' (Philippians 3:18). He is depicted as reminding the elders of Ephesus that 'for three years I never failed to keep you right, shedding tears over each one of you' (Acts 20:31). Paul was no sentimentalist, turning a blind eye to the shortcomings and failures of his people. But when he loved them, he loved them with a very affectionate human heart. Or, as he himself put it, loved them with the tenderness of Jesus Christ himself.

And yet Paul's ministry was far from being all sunshine. His experience of ministry was the familiar human mix of anywhere, anytime. There was elation and pride as in writing to Thessalonika; Paul is so happy with his people that he can brush aside his own 'troubles and sorrows' (I Thessalonians 3:7). But elation is only one segment of Paul's total apostolic experience. There is perplexity and blazing anger as Paul addresses himself to the problems of the church in Galatia. There are divisions to be deplored and abuses to be reproved as he writes I Corinthians; it is an illustration of what he himself calls 'my anxiety for all the churches' (II Corinthians 11:28). The Second Letter to the Corinthians finds Paul depressed, discouraged and bitterly hurt because he feels that he has been rejected by his converts in Corinth who, apparently, had welcomed instead to their hearts 'counterfeit apostles, they are dishonest workmen disguised as apostles of Christ' (II Corinthians 11:13). In Philippians, Paul, uncertain whether he may be released or executed, writes a brave Letter full of hope and joy. But behind the brave words you can sense the chill of fear: nothing to be ashamed of if Christ was afraid in the Garden. Joy, hope, fear, anger, elation, worry, perplexity, near-despair; all are in Paul's Letters because they were all in Paul's ministry.

What did Paul do with them? According to the fable, Midas turned everything he touched, ordinary everyday things, into gold. Paul took the ordinary everyday experiences of ministry, the pleasant as well as the painful, and turned all of them into loving. It is a recurring pattern in the Pauline Letters.

He is, for instance, annoyed with the Christian community in Corinth as he begins I Corinthians. There is dissension and division among them: some for Cephas, some for Paul, some for Apollos. As well there are abuses at the Eucharistic meeting, a notorious case of incest and an unchristian eagerness for litigation in the Roman courts. All these are simmering in Paul's mind as matter for rebuke and correction; and Paul begins almost fiercely: 'Was it Paul that was crucified for you? Were you baptised in the name of Paul?' (I Corinthians 1:13). But the severity doesn't last. In the third chapter he is back to the mother imagery of I Thessalonians, a mother feeding and looking after her own children. Very small and helpless children, 'I treated you as sensual men, still infants in Christ. What I fed you with was milk, not solid food, for you were not ready for it; and indeed you are still not ready for it' (I Corinthians 3:1–2). In the next chapter father-imagery replaces mother-imagery.

> I am saying all this, not to make you ashamed but to bring you, as my dearest children, to your senses. You might have thousands of guardians in Christ, but not more than one father and it was I who begot you in Christ Jesus by preaching you the Good News (I Corinthians 4:14–16).

But, mother-imagery or father-imagery, it is impossible to miss the tenderness, recalling the tenderness of Yahweh at the end of the Book of Jonah, 'And am I not to feel sorry for Nineveh, the great city, in which there are more than a hundred and twenty thousand people who cannot tell their right hand from their left' (Jonah 4:11). That is how Paul feels about the Corinthians. They are sinful, erring, troublesome—yes. But in the end they are pitiful little chil-

151

dren, unable as yet to tell their right hand from their left. They must be scolded. But above all they must be mothered.

When we meet him again at the beginning of II Corinthians, Paul is a broken man, 'the things we had to undergo in Asia were more of a burden than we could carry, so that we despaired of coming through alive' (II Corinthians 1:8). Paul was exhausted and tempted to discouragement. As this most human of Letters goes on, the reasons for exhaustion and discouragement emerge more clearly. Endless travelling, constant danger, opposition and persecution: Paul describes them vividly in Chapter 11. There was his daily preoccupation, his 'anxiety for all the churches' (II Corinthians 11:28). And there was more. For running through this Letter from beginning to end (if it is a single Letter) is the pain of rejection. Partly because of some misunderstanding about a journey Paul was supposed to make to them and didn't, the Corinthians, his very dear children as he saw them, had rejected him in favour of pseudo-apostles, 'if Satan himself goes disguised as an angel of light, there is no need to be surprised when his servants, too, disguise themselves as the servants of righteousness' (II Corinthians 11:14–15). Paul is furious and savagely sarcastic, 'Is there anything of which you have had less than the other churches have had, except that I have not myself been a burden on you? For this unfairness please forgive me' (II Corinthians 12:13). Exasperation, disappointment and a lacerated heart—all bubble up unpredictably in the course of this most inconsistent of Letters. And yet it remains uniquely the Letter of a lover.

> I may have hurt you, but if so I have hurt the only people who could give me any pleasure. ... I am sure you all know that I could never be happy unless you were. When I wrote to you, in deep distress and anguish of mind, and in tears, it was not to make you feel hurt but to let you know how much love I have for you (II Corinthians 2:1–4).

That is near the beginning of the Letter. Towards the end, after ten chapters containing a good deal of anger and expostulation we find Paul again using the language of the lover. 'It is you I want, not your possessions. ... I am perfectly willing to spend what I have, and to be expended, in the interests of your souls. Because I love

you more, must I be loved the less?' (II Corinthians 12:14–15.)
It is the same pattern in Galatians. As the Letter opens we meet
Paul at his angriest; so angry that he does not even give them his
normal greeting of peace. Paul makes no attempt at all to conceal
his chagrin. 'I am astonished at the promptness with which you
have turned away from the . . . Good News' (Galatians 1:6). Halfway through the Letter he again expresses his bewilderment and
dismay, 'Are you people in Galatia mad? Has someone put a spell
on you?' (Galatians 3:1.) Paul is angry, perplexed, even astonished.
But, Paul being Paul, it cannot last. 'My little children! I must go
through the pain of giving you birth all over again, until Christ is
formed in you. I wish I were with you now so that I could know
exactly what to say; as it is, I have no idea what to do for the best'
(Galatians 4:19–20).
The Letter to Philippi helps to complete the picture. In II Corinthians Paul had assured his Christian neophytes that he was
willing to spend himself and be spent on their behalf; to give them
unsparingly his life while it lasted. In Philippians, he tells them
how happy he will be to give them his life when it ends. That may
well be soon. For Paul, in prison, is uncertain of the outcome,
freedom or summary execution. It is a Letter remarkably free from
reproach or criticism although some of each is there. It is natural
that criticism should be muted here. This is, or well might be, a
last farewell Letter to some of his most loyal friends; hardly the
place, therefore, to say things that will hurt. Paul seems afraid that
they might fail to understand just how much they mean to him,
'You have a permanent place in my heart, and God knows how
much I miss you all, loving you as Christ Jesus loves you' (Philippians 1:7–8). And how had Jesus Christ loved them? 'Even to
accepting death, death on a cross' (Philippians 2:8). That, no doubt,
is in Paul's mind when he goes on to write, 'And then, if my blood
has to be shed as part of your own sacrifice and offering—which is
your faith—I shall still be happy and rejoice with all of you, and
you must be just as happy and rejoice with me' (Philippians
2:17–18). Ready and even happy to express his love, in the image
of Christ, by suffering for his Christians—that theme surfaces again
in Colossians, 'It makes me happy to suffer for you, as I am suffering
now, and in my own body to do what I can to make up for all that

153

has still to be undergone by Christ for the sake of his body, the Church' (Colossians 1:24). It is this, the human experience of fear and suffering, that Paul above all hopes to touch and, by touching, to turn it into loving. Catherine of Siena was so right in calling him *That Lover, Paul.*

It is, however, a view of Paul seldom encountered in the popular mind today. The Paul many Christian people seem to think of spontaneously is Paul the crabbed or the cantankerous. This is particularly true of many Christian women. They think immediately of the Paul who was fussy and impenetrable about what kind of head-dress ladies should wear in church. He was also brief and brusque about a feminine contribution to the on-going Christian debate, 'Women are to remain quiet at meetings since they have no permission to speak . . . If they have any questions to ask, they should ask their husbands at home' (I Corinthians 14:34–5). Not popular today either, and perhaps not always fully implemented, is the concise instruction, 'Wives, give way to your husbands, as you should in the Lord' (Colossians 3:18). In this area also the Pastoral Letters probably reflect Paul's own outlook, and female enthusiasm is limited for some comments on the world of fashion, 'Women are to wear suitable clothes and to be dressed quietly and modestly, without braided hair or gold and jewellery or expensive clothes' (I Timothy 2:9). The boutiques are unlikely to take him as their patron. The same Letter is scathing on young widows, 'They learn how to be idle and go around from house to house; and then, not merely idle, they learn to be gossips and meddlers in other people's affairs, and to chatter when they would be better keeping quiet' (I Timothy 5:13). Passages like these make it understandable that for many Christian women and some men Paul comes across as an unsympathetic figure.

It is important to examine to what extent these utterances are time-conditioned and what relevance they therefore may or may not have in our changed world. This examination can do something to put the unpopular Pauline utterances in perspective. Such an examination, however, is outside my present purpose. But, granting that these and similar statements of Paul are very much time-conditioned, I still think it true to say that Paul could be, on certain topics, somewhat crabbed and cantankerous; that sometimes he must have seemed difficult to those who worked closely with him, and occasionally impossible. Which is to say that he was a human being, with his own oddities and idiosyncrasies. Unfortunately it is this, the somewhat acrimonious Paul, Paul of the warts, that is most familiar in our day to the Christian imagination. The warts were, indeed, real. But I hope it will not seem blasphemous if I borrow the words of Francis Thompson and say that they were the warts of this tremendous lover. The anger, exasperation, touchiness and the rest—these were, if you like, the immediate spontaneous reactions of a very sensitive and highly strung man before they were transmuted into loving. In a poem called 'The Lesson for Today' Robert Frost has a final stanza that runs like this,

I hold your doctrine of Memento Mori
And were an epitaph to be my story
I'd have a short one ready for my own
I would have written of me on my stone
I had a lover's quarrel with the world.

A lover's quarrel can be tempestuous and the language intemperate. Frost's final line sums up for me a good deal about Paul. He had a lover's quarrel with the world.

The most important lesson, then, to be learned from Paul the Missionary—and in the present self-vision of the Church, every Christian is called to be in some way a missionary—is that if we are to preach what Christ preached, we must try to love as Christ loved. The professional missionary of today must indeed garb himself in many skills and techniques unknown to Paul. If, like Paul, he carries the Christian message to other races and peoples, he must try, while remaining what he is, to clothe himself in the customs and culture of those to whom he goes. But Paul would want to say also to him, indeed especially to him, what he wrote to the Colossians, 'Over all these clothes, to keep them together and complete them, put on love' (Colossians 3:14). Equally he would want to say to the missionaries of any age what he wrote to the Ephesians that they should be 'planted in love and built on love' (Ephesians 3:17). And if Paul were choosing from his own Letters just three words to sum up all he would wish to say to the missionary, I personally have no doubt what three words he would choose. He would go once more to Ephesians and say to us, 'Walk in love' (Ephesians 5:2. RSV). This *has* to be the pattern of Paul because it was the pattern of Christ. I know of no better words to describe Christ's mission from the Father than the words with which John introduces the Passion of Christ, 'Having loved his own who were in the world, he loved them to the end' (John 13:1. RSV). Neither do I know better words to describe the ideal of the missionary.

Ama et fac quod vis (Love and do what you like) . . . The phrase from Augustine, even though of wider Christian application, admirably sums up the central thrust of the missionary vocation. If the missionary, for all his human failures, is able to say with Paul in Philippians, 'You have a permanent place in my heart, and God knows how much I miss you all, loving you as Christ Jesus loves you' (Philippians 1:7–8), then most other things will take care of themselves. A Japanese Bishop spoke to me in Tokyo about a missionary in Japan who never had an opportunity to learn properly the appallingly difficult Japanese language, 'It is true he may not speak our language very well. But he has something more important. He has the language of the· heart. And the Japanese understand the language of the heart.' Paul too, for all his irritability and explosiveness, had the language of the heart. And people understood. That, no doubt, explains one of the most human passages in the Acts of the Apostles, at the end of the farewell address to the elders of Ephesus,

> When he had finished speaking he knelt down with them all and prayed. By now they were all in tears; they put their arms around Paul's neck and kissed him; what saddened them most was his saying that they would never see his face again. Then they escorted him to the ship (Acts 20:36–8).

Somewhere in the missionary world a scene like that is re-enacted every week, perhaps every day. Except that nowadays they escort him, or her, to the airport.

Love and do what you like. It sounds simple as the basic recipe for the missionary task. But of course it is not simple at all. For *real* loving has to be translated into real people, real situations, real problems, real conflicts—and must become as diverse as these. Somebody or other has said that the only real heroism is taking the world as it is and loving it. It is not a bad description of what it is to be a missionary. However diverse the shapes of our loving, all will demand self-emptying on the model of the Christ Paul talks about in Philippians, who 'emptied himself, to assume the condition of a slave' (Philippians 2:7). This self-emptying love will vary enormously with special vocation. It will take very different shapes in the medical missionary sister, the ministerial priest or the dedicated lay missionary. But if it is modelled on the love of Paul, and beyond that on the love of Christ, it stretches out to *all* without exception, 'there are no more distinctions between Jew and Greek, slave and free, male and female, but all of you are one in Christ Jesus' (Galatians 3:28). This is of crucial importance in the face of the bitter divisions of society often facing the missionary today. He must be close to the poor, identified with the poor, and defender of the oppressed against the oppressor. But when he criticises or opposes the oppressor, he must still be able to make his own the words of Paul to the Corinthians, 'When I wrote to you, in deep distress and anguish of mind, and in tears, it was not to make you feel hurt but to let you know how much love I have for you' (II Corinthians 2:4). Or, as Paul put it elsewhere, 'You are not to regard him as an enemy but a brother in need of correction' (II Thessalonians 3:15). Not simple and certainly not easy. In other words it is Christianity. Paul VI has reminded us of all this in a forgotten sentence of *Evangelii Nuntiandi*. Having sketched the main features of the missionary vocation in our day he goes on to say, 'the work of evangelization presupposes in the evangelizer an ever-increasing love for those whom he is evangelizing' (*EN* 79). When it comes to the heart of apostolate Paul of Tarsus and Paul VI speak with one clear voice. Both ask us to preach Christ 'out of nothing but love, as they know that this is my invariable way of defending the gospel' (Philippians 1:16).

Out of nothing but love! It is, indeed, simplification. But it is the simplification of the Gospels. Perhaps we need to bring that kind of simplification to our understanding of the missionary role today. Over the past decades we have analysed it, discussed it, defined it, redefined it; we have learned to present it in complicated and even

157

sophisticated terms. All this is obviously good; we work in a complicated world and we must respect the shape of reality. But, with all the complexities, is there some danger of forgetting the simplicity at the centre?

For, like Paul, we really have only one thing to proclaim to a bewildered humanity, and it is not of course his or ours at all, 'the love of God made visible in Christ Jesus our Lord' (Romans 8:39). It would be a tragedy if we missionaries, of all people, had to be reminded of this by contemporary thinkers and writers, hardly calling themselves Christian at all. Solzhenitsyin immediately comes to mind. In Christ this love was visible, perceptible, almost tangible. In our humbler way this should be true also of us. Like Christ, each of us must be Sacrament of God. To put it in less theological language, any good salesman brings samples of his wares. As samples, we missionaries bring ourselves. People will be less impressed by the things we say than the samples we are.

This means that about the most important treatise on missiology was written nearly two thousand years ago and consists of a little over a thousand words. It is of course the thirteenth chapter of I Corinthians. Paul was, no doubt, thinking partly of himself, perhaps mainly of himself when he wrote the opening lines, 'If I have all the eloquence of men or of angels, but speak without love, I am simply a gong booming or a cymbal clashing' (I Corinthians 13:1). If we missionaries want to be something better than '*booming gong*' or '*clashing cymbal*', Paul points the clear way. 'You must want love more than anything else' (I Corinthians 14:1).

POSTSCRIPT

There is only one *City of God* and one Augustine. He would, however, look on with benignity when the poor borrow from his immense riches. So I reproduce here the words with which he closes the *City of God*,

> I am done. With God's help, I have kept my promise. This, I think, is all that I promised to do when I began this huge work. From all who think that I have said either too little or too much, I beg pardon; and those who are satisfied I ask, not to thank me, but to join me in rejoicing and in thanking God. Amen.

INDEX OF BIBLICAL REFERENCES

163

Other Orbis books . . .

THE MEANING OF MISSION

José Comblin

"This very readable book has made me think, and I feel it will be useful for anyone dealing with their Christian role of mission and evangelism." *New Review of Books and Religion*
ISBN 0-88344-304-X CIP   *Cloth $6.95*

THE GOSPEL OF PEACE AND JUSTICE

Catholic Social Teaching Since Pope John

Presented by Joseph Gremillion

"Especially valuable as a resource. The book brings together 22 documents containing the developing social teaching of the church from *Mater et Magistra* to Pope Paul's 1975 *Peace Day Message on Reconciliation.* I watched the intellectual excitement of students who used Gremillion's book in a justice and peace course I taught last summer, as they discovered a body of teaching on the issues they had defined as relevant. To read Gremillion's overview and prospectus, a meaty introductory essay of some 140 pages, is to be guided through the sea of social teaching by a remarkably adept navigator."
National Catholic Reporter
"An authoritative guide and study aid for concerned Catholics and others." *Library Journal*
ISBN 0-88344-165-9   *Cloth $15.95*
ISBN 0-88344-166-7   *Paper $8.95*

THEOLOGY IN THE AMERICAS

Papers of the 1975 Detroit Conference

Edited by Sergio Torres and John Eagleson

"A pathbreaking book from and about a pathbreaking theological conference, *Theology in the Americas* makes a major contribution to ecumenical theology, Christian social ethics and liberation movements in dialogue." *Fellowship*
ISBN 0-88344-479-8 CIP   *Cloth $12.95*
ISBN 0-88344-476-3   *Paper $5.95*

THE CHURCH AND POWER IN BRAZIL

Charles Antoine

"This is a book which should serve as a basis of discussion and further study by all who are interested in the relationship of the Church to contemporary governments, and all who believe that the Church has a vital role to play in the quest for social justice." *Worldmission*
ISBN 0-88344-062-8   *Paper $4.95*

HISTORY AND
THE THEOLOGY OF LIBERATION

Enrique Dussel

"The book is easy reading. It is a brilliant study of what may well be or should be the future course of theological methodology."
Religious Media Today
ISBN 0-88344-179-9   *Cloth $8.95*
ISBN 0-88344-180-2   *Paper $4.95*

DOM HELDER CAMARA

José de Broucker

"De Broucker, an internationally recognized journalist, develops a portrait, at once intimate, comprehensive and sympathetic, of the Archbishop of Olinda and Recife, Brazil, whose championship of political and economic justice for the hungry, unorganized masses of his country and all Latin America has aroused world attention."
America
ISBN 0-88344-099-7   *Cloth $6.95*

THE DESERT IS FERTILE

Dom Helder Camara

"Camara's brief essays and poems are arresting for their simplicity and depth of vision, and are encouraging because of the realistic yet quietly hopeful tone with which they argue for sustained action toward global justice." *Commonweal*
ISBN 0-88344-078-4   *Cloth $3.95*

MARX AND THE BIBLE

José Miranda

"An inescapable book which raises more questions than it answers, which will satisfy few of us, but will not let us rest easily again. It is an attempt to utilize the best tradition of Scripture scholarship to understand the text when it is set in a context of human need and misery."

Walter Brueggemann, in Interpretation

ISBN 0-88344-306-6   *Cloth $8.95*
ISBN 0-88344-307-4   *Paper $4.95*

BEING AND THE MESSIAH

The Message of Saint John

José Miranda

"This book could become the catalyst of a new debate on the Fourth Gospel. Johannine scholarship will hotly debate the 'terrifyingly revolutionary thesis that this world of contempt and oppression can be changed into a world of complete selflessness and unrestricted mutual assistance.' Cast in the framework of an analysis of contemporary philosophy, the volume will prove a classic of Latin American theology." *Frederick Herzog, Duke University Divinity School*

ISBN 0-88344-027-X CIP   *Cloth $8.95*
ISBN 0-88344-028-8   *Paper $4.95*

THE GOSPEL IN SOLENTINAME

Ernesto Cardenal

"Upon reading this book, I want to do so many things—burn all my other books which at best seem like hay, soggy with mildew. I now know who (not what) is the church and how to celebrate church in the eucharist. The dialogues are intense, profound, radical. *The Gospel in Solentiname* calls us home."

Carroll Stuhlmueller, National Catholic Reporter

ISBN 0-88344-170-5   *Vol. 1 Paper $4.95*
ISBN 0-88344-167-5   *Vol. 2 Cloth $6.95*

THEOLOGY FOR A NOMAD CHURCH

Hugo Assmann

"A new challenge to contemporary theology which attempts to show that the theology of liberation is not just a fad, but a new political dimension which touches every aspect of Christian existence."

Publishers Weekly

ISBN 0-88344-493-3   *Cloth $7.95*
ISBN 0-88344-494-1   *Paper $4.95*

FREEDOM MADE FLESH

The Mission of Christ and His Church

Ignacio Ellacuría

"Ellacuría's main thesis is that God's saving message and revelation are historical, that is, that the proclamation of the gospel message must possess the same historical character that revelation and salvation history do and that, for this reason, it must be carried out in history and in a historical way." *Cross and Crown*

ISBN 0-88344-140-3   *Cloth $8.95*
ISBN 0-88344-141-1   *Paper $4.95*

THE LIBERATION OF THEOLOGY

Juan Luis Segundo

"It is a remarkable book in terms of its boldness in confronting the shortcomings of the Christian tradition and in terms of the clarity of vision provided by the hermeneutic of liberation. Segundo writes with ease whether dealing with the sociological, theological, or political roots of liberation. His is a significant addition to the recent work of Cone, Alves, Moltmann, and Gutiérrez because it compels the movement to interrogate its own theological foundations. A necessary addition, in one of the more fruitful directions of contemporary theology, it is appropriate for graduate, undergraduate, or clerical readers." *Choice*

"The book makes for exciting reading and should not be missing in any theological library." *Library Journal*

ISBN 0-88344-285-X CIP   *Cloth $10.95*
ISBN 0-88344-286-8   *Paper $6.95*

CHRISTIANS, POLITICS
AND VIOLENT REVOLUTION

J.G. Davies

"Davies argues that violence and revolution are on the agenda the world presents to the Church and that consequently the Church must reflect on such problems. This is a first-rate presentation, with Davies examining the question from every conceivable angle."

National Catholic News Service
ISBN 0-88344-061-X   *Paper $4.95*

CHRISTIAN POLITICAL THEOLOGY
A MARXIAN GUIDE

Joseph Petulla

"Petulla presents a fresh look at Marxian thought for the benefit of Catholic theologians in the light of the interest in this subject which was spurred by Vatican II, which saw the need for new relationships with men of all political positions." *Journal of Economic Literature*
ISBN 0-88344-060-1   *Paper $4.95*

THE NEW CREATION:
MARXIST AND CHRISTIAN?

José María González-Ruiz

"A worthy book for lively discussion."
The New Review of Books and Religion
ISBN 0-88344-327-9 CIP   *Cloth $6.95*

CHRISTIANS AND SOCIALISM

Documentation of the Christians for
Socialism Movement in Latin America

Edited by John Eagleson

"Compelling in its clear presentation of the issue of Christian commitment in a revolutionary world." *The Review of Books and Religion*
ISBN 0-88344-058-X   *Paper $4.95*

THE CHURCH AND
THIRD WORLD REVOLUTION

Pierre Bigo

"Heavily documented, provocative yet reasonable, this is a testament, demanding but impressive." *Publishers Weekly*
ISBN 0-88344-071-7 CIP   *Cloth $8.95*
ISBN 0-88344-072-5   *Paper $4.95*

WHY IS THE THIRD WORLD POOR?

Piero Gheddo

"An excellent handbook on the Christian understanding of the development process. Gheddo looks at both the internal and external causes of underdevelopment and how Christians can involve themselves in helping the third world." *Provident Book Finder*
ISBN 0-88344-757-6   *Paper $4.95*

POLITICS AND SOCIETY
IN THE THIRD WORLD

Jean-Yves Calvez

"This frank treatment of economic and cultural problems in developing nations suggests the need for constant multiple attacks on the many fronts that produce problems in the human situation."
                                                The Christian Century
ISBN 0-88344-389-9   *Cloth $6.95*

A THEOLOGY OF LIBERATION

Gustavo Gutiérrez

"The movement's most influential text." *Time*
    "The most complete presentation thus far available to English readers of the provocative theology emerging from the Latin American Church." *Theological Studies*
    "North Americans as well as Latin Americans will find so many challenges and daring insights that they will, I suggest, rate this book one of the best of its kind ever written." *America*
ISBN 0-88344-477-1   *Cloth $7.95*
ISBN 0-88344-478-X   *Paper $4.95*